ALL THE WOMEN IN MY BRAIN

ALL THE
WOMEN
IN MY
BRAIN

And Other Concerns

Betty Gilpin

FLATIRON
BOOKS
NEW YORK

ALL THE WOMEN IN MY BRAIN. Copyright © 2022 by Betty Gilpin. All rights reserved. Printed in the United States of America. For information, address Flatiron Books, 120 Broadway, New York, NY 10271.

www.flatironbooks.com

Designed by Donna Sinisgalli Noetzel

The Library of Congress Cataloging-in-Publication Data is available upon request.

ISBN 978-1-250-79578-6 (hardcover)
ISBN 978-1-250-84615-0 (ebook)

Our books may be purchased in bulk for promotional, educational, or business use. Please contact your local bookseller or the Macmillan Corporate and Premium Sales Department at 1-800-221-7945, extension 5442, or by email at MacmillanSpecialMarkets@macmillan.com.

First Edition: 2022

10 9 8 7 6 5 4 3 2 1

For you, my secret favorite

CONTENTS

AUTHOR'S NOTE

This is a true story, though some names have been changed.

ALL THE WOMEN IN MY BRAIN

—

1

AHEM

—

Dear reader,

Picture a mute feather woman. She's essentially a bloodless meerkat recluse working as a night janitor for an apothecary. She does helpful things like apologize to the sun and lie facedown on census day so she's not on record for being alive. Now ask her to stand in the center of a farmer's market and pop-belt reasons why she loves herself and should be elected mayor.

This is me writing a book.

To write you a letter listing reasons why you should be interested in my brain is to pour curdled milk on my personal bill of rights, which for years decreed that the shadows and unsent-idea emails were my mental *Cheers* bar.

But I'm writing a book. I'm writing a book, and the women in my brain are hyperventilating.

Some are in pilled sweaters meaning well, some are building forts or writing terrible poems, some have blood in their teeth and are throwing a cantaloupe through a store window. All of these brainwomen are different. Most of them are afraid. Many of them stand sentry at the door, warning the other women of the dangers of bravery and action. Lipstick for the bodega might send the poisonous message that you love yourself—suggesting that your ideas are worthy is identity suicide. It's bagpipes at a library. It's a selfie at a funeral. It would kill us, plead the brain-women. Leave the hand-raising to the women without cereal in their bra. Delete this paragraph.

Well, that was the first thirty years of my life. Then a strange combination of personal and world events gently then violently shifted my brainwomen, sedating some and birthing others. To my shock, some of the veterans announced their desire to phase out from twenty-four-hour megaphone duty and become a nap-prone member of the board. One woman stood up from leaning against a supply closet and out fell another—bound, gagged, and kicking her pantyhosed legs at the women who'd locked her away.

I feel a shift. There are things we do to protect ourselves as ladies that make sense when we're twelve or twenty-five, but now with things like retinols and Donalds we no longer need those brainwomen's help to feel shame. So I'm baking some of those women an Ambien Bundt cake and writing this E. E. Cummings wedding toast of a book to you before they wake up.

Of course, I love those brainwomen, too. Every time they held me back from running at something, I saw a different color of the world. Something I would have missed if I'd ignored them. While many of my braver friends seemed to run with a spear at the horizon, I sat with binoculars and a notebook. And now, before I suddenly throw my computer in an acid bath, I'd like to present my field notes.

———

My name is Betty. Sorry, as an actor I've been conditioned to exchange deepest fears and traumas before names. If the brain is a house, I like to get right to the terrifying attic and haunted second bathroom of truths and just bypass the vestibule of small talk and boundaries. Don't worry, this won't be an actor memoir. I don't have any delusions that the octogenarian auctioneers who have seen my Off-Broadway theatre canon are clamoring for my childhood timeline. Nor do I think the gentlemen who send me eight-by-ten printouts of my own breasts to sign are petitioning for my book—I'm not aware that they know I can read. But now that there's been a small brain earthquake and I'm coughing dramatically through the smoke, I see that all my experiences as a sometimes-working actor have been a perfect allegory for being a woman in this world. Having to cycle through identities to give whoever is in front of you the girl they want, feeling like you have to audition for the job you already have, having a quarter of the time that men do to achieve your dreams before your tits are in your shoes and the government deems you disgusting and banishes you to eat sleeves of tear-soaked saltines in bed until you die.

I have been doing actor weirdness professionally for fifteen years. Most of that has consisted of trying. Trying to make smaller my facial expressions, choices, and curves—all of which were too big to play sexy aunt with laundry or slutty neighbor with question. Trying not to listen to the business when it told me the things that were valuable about myself were not my imagination and darkness but my youth and cleavage. Trying not to feel shame for wanting things, and battling the anvil-anklets of depression and anxiety while walking through the world as an apologizing Barbie. Trying.

And then sometimes, in the dead of night, in a hamster-on-deathbed whisper, I do something illegal. Do you? Do you ever wonder if you could . . . never mind. It's gross to type.

(TYPE IT, COWARD.)

Listen. I could write a dissertation on the *blegh* of my face and the *suck* of my ways. But also of course is that other thing, buried in all the *no* and *sorry*.

There is something inside you, and something different inside me, and in Al Roker and Elian Gonzalez and your dentist, that is insane and obscure and extraordinary. And yours. A tiny little pinprick of light. It's buried under lead bags of fear and oh well. Sometimes you think maybe it doesn't exist. Its externalization instructions are written in a dead language. Maybe one time you were given the chance to unearth it and let it float out, and nothing happened. You take that as proof it was all in your head, so you never try again. Maybe you're convinced that unless the world acknowledges your light as extraordinary, then it doesn't matter. It was never real.

Somewhere along the way I got too tired to hate myself *all* the time. And looked in the mirror and thought, *you fuck, you have to try.* I don't know what it looks like, but there's something in there that has to come out. Something, to use a horrible word, "special."

Have asked publisher to use puke-proof paper

I am at the point where the caterpillar asks for a pretransformation cigarette break. She briefly wonders if she could turn into an eagle, or instead position herself to get pancaked by a Hyundai. We all have it at some point: the horrific adult realization that no one is going to hold you down, cut you open, and forcibly extract your centimeter-tall scroll of inner magnificence for the world to read. It's in your hands to decide your fate as magic or sweat-pants. What once were personality quirks that made your emails more relatable are now sandbags against the door to potential. So many of us feel like we are designed for Greek circumstances but are given Ikea boxes to put them in. Emotionally, this book is an opportunity to sit together on the floor of Grand Central, turn our purses inside out, and simultaneously shit our pants. (I both know exactly what that means and have also lost the thread.)

No—what I mean is this. So many of us wait until the hallway or journal or car to open the compartment where we hide our ugly and our majesty. I want this book to scalpel out the darkness and ask if it looks like yours. Then I want to coax out the lice-sized brainwoman who believes we are meant for the moon and ask her to speak, too. I want to write about being afraid and grabbing the spear anyway, sobbing and peeing and sprinting at the horizon.

2

SALEM OR BARBIE

Are we ready for more metaphors? Who needs water? Oops, we lost a reader. Bye, Meredith!

For those left:

Do you ever look at our generation and roar, "Fuck *yes!*" Then squint at something alarming and whisper, "Oh *no.*"

Listen—now is great. Feminism is everywhere; feminism is Beanie Babies. *You're welcome!* we post. It is, of course, not our *welcome* to *you're*. We modern Braveheart McDormands had very little to do with it. Centuries of women before us whispered *no* into hoop skirts, then growled it into bloomers, then screamed it braless into megaphones. The whispers and growls and screams were passed down like woke diabetes. Each next little baby girl was born with eyes wider and wider open to her own shackled potential. And now us! The official patriarchy antidote carrier pigeons!

The problem is it's . . . well . . . it's *us*.

In my humble, probably wrong, select-all-delete opinion, we womenfolk today are faced with a decision: Salem or Barbie. We can either rip off the internal trapdoor that your Alanis Plath of Arc has been suffocating under or cement over it and instead luxuriate in a Hello Kitty porny Instagram-filtered cell where the validation is better than heroin and the thoughts are shorter than Mickey Rooney. (HEY-OH!) Both chambers exist in the female psyche. Both celebrate polar-opposite qualities of womanness. Both need your help to survive. Both are disgusted by the other. Much of my life is spent frantically commuting between these two chambers. I am terrified that if I don't maintain a steady to-and-fro, the trapdoor will be sealed forever, and I'll be stuck on the wrong side. The casual news is each has the power to kill us. So before we choose one, let's examine the candidates.

Under the trapdoor within us, the Salem chamber is fucking wild. It is a churning sea of monsters in your gut. It is a frothing black ocean of your fullest, darkest, most terrifying potential. Peer down there and see all of your ancient ancestors screaming poems into the dark waves. Look! There's a group of sorceresses building a telescope out of your childhood traumas. And there! A she-gargoyle in a bathrobe is writing a song about sixth grade and genocide. OK, wow, she's giving birth to a knife.

Everywhere here, pain and experience become windows and ideas. Used and fed correctly, this is your superpower. The trapdoor kept open to this part of you means the monsters can make meaningful things that etch your existence into the "who was here" universe log. When used in your relationships, you let yourself feel the full pain and beauty of *really* knowing someone, and being known. It is spectacular. Open the trapdoor and see the big questions float up to you: Who am I? Who are you? Where is God? Why all this?

As a child, it was easy to be here. As a child, that's all there was. I swam in it all day. *I'm going to run until the recess frost soaks through my Keds, because I'm a rabid justice mercenary! I'm going to use all purples and browns in art today because that's what my monster soup is screeching for, and I need to see where it goes. I don't have time to think about the tomato sauce on my face—I'm conducting a séance with a dead mouse.* I was a tangled-hair rage angel who screamed, "AYE AYE" from apple trees. I kicked my unshaven legs around like electric spaghetti. I picked my clothes based on colors *I* liked and what priestess or scallywag I might embody that day. There was no apology, no checkpoint between my brain and the world, to make sure my output was acceptable.

Then it changed.

Slowly but surely inconveniences like tits and trauma peppered themselves into my life, and wearing a lobster pot on my head while charging at an oak tree was no longer socially viable. The monster soup became a complicated place to exist in. I started to see myself from a bird's-eye view. *Betty, when you're loud, you're too much. When you wear purple, you're too much. When you have sauce on your face, it means you're not invited to Jonah's bar mitzvah, and that means loneliness.* The mirror suddenly became important, something scrappy-warrior-me would only use for the ugly-face game.

Imagination and bravery became less useful as a growing girl. Suddenly life was a point system where things that were once my lifeblood were now worth near zero.

In middle school I realized that not all of my monsters & co.

were laughing. Some of them were becoming terrifying. I felt a connection to things that scared me. I sensed a deeper weirder darkness churning that I didn't understand, huge questions and feelings that I had no tools to address. Instead of wanting to build a mud castle, now the monster soup wanted to explore suffering and existence and the sky.

I was disappointed to see there was no time for those things. It became apparent that my highest purpose as a twelve-year-old girl was not to ask questions and externalize the weird to see where it led but instead to soften and cutesify my identity to submit for acceptance. I had been wrong: I was not an alchemist. I was a tank top.

So I began heartbreaking internal renovations. I let the monsters know that while I *so* valued their contribution to my multicolored feast of a life, I saw it was safer for them to be muted. Avoiding eye contact with a gorgon, I closed the trapdoor.

On top of that trapdoor, I did what girls have to do. I built the Barbie cell.

The Barbie cell is a checkpoint between your power and the world, a filter between your weird and the cafeteria. Here your dreams and sentences that drift up from the gremlins who once designed your playdates are now passed through the trapdoor and vetted in this cell; picked over for ugly; scrubbed clean of the dangers of idiosyncrasy, volume turned down; and sent out into the world with an apology disclaimer. Sure, sometimes you open the trapdoor and dip into the monster soup alone in your room or with a rare friend whose cardigan you're not copying; but otherwise, the Salem chamber is suddenly useless.

Useless, and sometimes just . . . too painful. It's not always fun to keep the trapdoor open. It means listening to music that makes you remember things you'd rather not. It means getting through the book that's making your brain light up with imagery but Jesus God this chapter is a boring downer. It's watching the news to stay connected to the immense need of the whole world, which can be an impossible idea to hold in your brain while holding a pointless latte in your hand.

Keeping the trapdoor open means being uncomfortable and uncertain. It means treating the world as a question and yourself as a worthy seeker of answers. That can be wholly terrifying. Or immensely depressing. Or honestly? Just . . . boring. The modern attention span combined with our learned shame is a perfect excuse not to open the trapdoor that day. *Who am I to be a sorceress? I don't* want *to swim in the needle-water of my full capacity of aliveness today. I'd like to be a little less sad and work a little less hard. I don't* want *to know myself—I don't love what I've got so far.*

The solution is the Barbie cell.

Sitting on top of the trapdoor is a room where everything's *easy*. The Barbie cell is my pastel, cushioned den of sexy, delicious escape and distraction. Let me show you around. Here Princess Jasmine is making a Sour Patch Kid mosaic out of compliments I've received. A gaggle of vocal fry cartoon bunnies discuss aerobics and jeans. Over on the waterbed, a human cupcake scrolls Twitter, copying down opinions for me to recycle as my own at a dinner party, thereby rescuing me from the excruciating tedium of original thought. Over here a montage of kittens and my own achievements plays on a loop for me to escape to when my lunch partner is detailing their mother's illness: the vulnerability of a situation I can't control is painful and boring! Top-40-forget-life music is pumped in through Brazilian-waxed speakers—certainly no song with an actual instrument or thesis statement that would stir a memory and crack open the trapdoor.

I am tempted to live here forever, filling my brain with cotton candy smoke, smudging out the ugly.

I spent adolescence feeling like a vile dunce leper clawing at any semblance of acceptance. The postpuberty realization that my expirable qualities could achieve an open door or eye contact with little to no work felt like I'd discovered how to frack champagne. Pre-boobs, my journal was filled every night with (illegally bad) poems and emo-crazed paragraphs about What It All Meant. Less so when I realized it was more difficult to weave my journal into my outward identity as a woman, and easier to craft the illusion of a fuckable, trauma-less girl. Easier to stay in the Barbie cell, collect validation points as the cheap way to stay alive and needed, and let the Salem stuff be a secret.

Hide your darkness; show your belly button.

Then in the ultimate act of self-betrayal, I learned how to *sell* the darkness. I saw I could treat it as fodder for the character the Barbie cell wanted to convince the world I was. *Posing* with a journal at Starbucks but not actually *writing* in it. Pulling at my sleeves in performed angst, biting my lip and conjuring a sexy tear so the football player eating an exploded pen across the classroom would deign to consider masturbating to my mystery. The gargoyles and witches in my black ocean chamber wailed in horror as I stopped treating them like the portal to power, but instead a haunted warehouse only accessed when I needed Barbie-cell validation. I refurbished a plastic cutesier version for the vocal-fry princesses upstairs to sell for an eyebrow raise. Like some huckster salesman selling blow-up doll witches on the outskirts of Salem.

The trapdoor threatened to cement over forever.

Making my living as an actress has been a strange, frantic commute between these two chambers. I first became an actor exclusively because of the Salem shit. For most of the time, acting feels like you are an uninvited impostor troll, tap-dancing for an audience who you're convinced is silently begging you to stop and kill yourself. But every once in a trillion attempts, it feels like glorious haunted church. Reality shifts and your trapdoor is ripped off its hinges, and all the ghosts come out into the room and float. I'm suddenly all the things I was when I was seven, before apologies replaced questions. The monster soup is no longer an abandoned warehouse but a maniacal Amazonian Mardi Gras of ideas and visions. I feel my whole body pulse like a living weapon. And then a cell phone goes off in the audience, and I'm terrible again and the moment is over. But the monsters under the trapdoor are fat with feeding, elated and strong.

Sadly, as an actress, you often are not hired for the ghosty stuff but for the least interesting parts of yourself. The video game dowry qualities. Not for what you're capable of but for how you adorably *seem*. You're not a powerful chameleon interpreter. You are instead to hold a laundry basket or helpful lube near the *real* story: *him*.

The pursuit of an acting job involves an inordinate amount of time in the Barbie cell. After a few years of auditioning, I wondered if spending less time on charting the character's family tree and more time curling my hair would get me more work. (It did.) In drama school, being an actor meant sobbing in pajamas and attempting organ-shifting sorcery, probably with terrible results, but it felt like magic. In the real world, being an actress meant trying to Spanx and paint and squint myself into pretending

I have existed forever as a shy little Bond girl who will never age or fart. If I'm lucky, and the fake eyelashes get me the job, I can try to Trojan horse some of the ghosty stuff in on the third take. (They probably won't use it—too many weird faces.) Every audition is preceded by an hour of panicking about how to make myself less hideous. Every time I step on set it's after two hours of hair and makeup that morph me into a porny stranger. But it's the toll I have to pay to get to the monster soup. Get in the room by giving them what they want from the pink fantasy doll suite, then secretly pry open the trapdoor and be Medea with lip gloss.

What scares me is the temptation to stay in the former. As I type, I'm in this millisecond-long intersection of genetics and career where my tits and neck haven't committed suicide and the entertainment business has briefly deemed me acceptable to hire. It is too terrifying a question to ask the world, *Why am I allowed to play the sobbing wife? Is it the writhing witches who conjured the tears, or the perky-for-now tits on which those tears plop?*

It was years of lying in the grass conducting a cloud symphony with tiny dirty toes, then lonely preteen me asking those clouds for answers that made my favorite parts of me. The Barbie cell makes me forget. I get validation-drunk. Looking at a photo of me where my cheeks are artificially rosier and angle-ier, where my lips have been outlined a few centimeters fluffier, where my eyelids look like Van Gogh coughed on each of them and then a family of cashmere caterpillars took a group nap on my lashes and eyebrows, where my hair has been burned and torqued into that of a cartoon pony's, where my borrowed tailored clothes make me look like I just stepped off a boat where everyone fucks by the cheese plate, where the angle at which I'm standing and trick of the light make me look smaller and younger and my facial expression offers a blow job as a sexy tariff, looking at this photo . . . feels . . . so . . . fucking . . . good.

(Pause as I funnel Dramamine into Susan B. Anthony's grave.)

I don't have a public social media account as an actor. But I have played with death and searched my name on fecalstew.com: Twitter. Since the world spent my adolescence convincing me I was disgusting, now a handful of invisible Wi-Fi-owners deeming me fuckable feels like victory. Giddy from the win, I then open the trapdoor to call up goblins for a scene or an essay, but . . . wait. They're all flipping me off, on strike, having been ignored for weeks of lip gloss and self-deprecation. Filming a scene, I used to be able to conjure a creativity witch with a deep breath. Now I have to fight past Barbie-cell members reminding me the priority in this scene is not the fickle pursuit of catharsis but the opportunity to convince the world I'm gorgeous. Using the churning ocean of darkness and imagination within me to ask the universe a question is pointless, the Barbies insist. Much safer to just focus on sucking it in and ask the only question we women need worry about:

Do you love me?

The curse is that this question is the most addictive, distracting pursuit.

Do you love me?

It is the most tempting diversion from your own actualization, from your exploding into your fullest potential. If the choices are either to wade through a moat of pain and unknowing to a vague dream of a warrior self or to achieve guaranteed acceptance with no vulnerability or pain required . . . the latter sounds nicer. If you are feeling depressed and the monster soup feels like acid glue pudding, putting on Lycra and watching a Channing Ruffalo Pitt see you and walk into a parking meter is emotional Narcan. The inhabitants of the Barbie cell writhe with the hit of validation cocaine and command you to avoid bagels and books so that you may serve the highest purpose—to be worshipped. To be in favor. *This feels like power.* But the hit is so brief, the wave of acceptance gone in an instant, and self-hate and shame flood the Barbie cell like a septic explosion at Sephora.

Now, the horrific reveal. Behind the glitter-curtain is the Barbie cell's *true* creator—not the mirror-loving, gorgeous-forever, arms-open Beyoncé you thought was in charge but the Patriarchal Beast himself. *He* is at the controls. Terrified of the powers that gurgle and hiss under your trapdoor, he tries to convince you that your greatest purpose is begging for his love. *Keep your mouth shut and your life small. Better spend your days making sure your silence and sweaters hide the ugly lest anyone see you're a walking God-typo unworthy of love and Evites.*

It's difficult to pick up a sword when you hate yourself.

Yes, we should enjoy the ant-heartbeat of a second where we look like princesses, but not at the expense of abandoning the things that will make us queens. I don't want my worst nightmare to be wrinkles and irrelevance. I want it to be that I never listened to the witches' ideas before they gave up and stopped singing. I'm terrified that if I believe the beast when it tells me my magic comes from the things that will expire, then later when I sag and wilt and soft lighting is futile, and basement e-commenters no longer masturbate to airbrushed lie-pictures of me, and construction workers stop hooting and Hollywood stops calling, that only *then* will I frantically throw open the trapdoor for answers and purpose. I'll call down saying, "I love you! I'm sorry! I've missed you so much!" and all that will sound back is my own lonely echo. And I'll look up asking the Barbie cell for help, but they've gone, too—the beast pink-slipped the staff once I no longer had the wares to sell. And I'm left alone in an abandoned cavern, wondering how I'm going to spend the last forty years of my life.

So what is to be done? How do we kill the bro-beast inside before he kills us? How do we attempt actualization when the shame calls are still coming from inside the brain house? How do we eliminate the trapdoor altogether? Could the residents both above and below . . . collaborate? A terrifying and wonderful thought. Alone, I have no idea how to do this. But watching other women who do gives me strength to try. I watch with awe as some women reclaim things like beauty and sexuality as their own, both lasting much longer than a magazine tells them it does. I also marvel at women who can mute shame to let a dream take shape.

I want that. I want to someday smile at my silver hair in the mirror and then smile wider at a weird idea. An idea that had all the space it needed to float to the surface. And maybe my silver hair will even have a bow in it, because I loved myself enough to be deserving of both ideas and a bow.

And a sword.

3

MOM AND DAD

To explain away some of my blendered brain, you should know, my parents are actors. I remember thinking it was like they had Santa DNA. Theatre, mostly—those were the days before the internet could catapult your identity across state lines quicker than an unaffordable flight could. So in the nineties, New York actors mostly did plays about tense dinners and episodes of *Law and Order*. So that's what my parents did.

I was aware and proud of the hum of magic around their profession, smug that it was different from Isabel G's dad's job that seemed to mute his identity into Eeyore with a tie. But it also seemed normal to me, like it was our version of the family farm or donut shop. A shop I was desperate to inherit one day. Their carnie status also bled into our minivanned lives, infusing the mundane with grandeur and banana peels. Playdate guests were either enthralled and begged to return or exhausted and never came back.

If you're looking for a stern lawyer with a twinkle of understanding, or a regal patriarch who takes his tea on the veranda, or a crestfallen prince with his heart open and soul ready for vengeance, or a terrifying professor in the shadows with a dagger and thesaurus, consider my father. Gravitas is not an optional faucet, reader. It courses through one's veins whether you are center stage with a skull or murmuring an old monologue at a chili pot.

Most of us pronounce the word "stew" like "stoo." No. From my father, it is always "stieu." "Why" is not "wai." It's "hhwwhaieh." If you are seven and at our home for a sleepover, brace yourself for breakfast. The volume and severity with which my father lists cereal options *will* make you cry. Because it is not a droned, uncaffeinated, casual roster of brands. Nay, it is a mezzanine-slapping stadium announcement of the esteemed soldiers of morning, the consonants of "RAISIN BRAN" boxing your ears like aural muskets, a pause to fill the diaphragm and then "SPECIAL *K*" screamed like he's announcing the entrance of a one-legged war hero surprising his mother at a town raffle, "BROWN *SQUARE* KIND" valiantly boomed without irony (our strange family code for Wheat Chex), ". . . *TOTAL*" spoken with reverence as the most respected general to serve us but with a solemn understanding we would never choose it, and then finally ". . . C . . . T . . . *C!*" the grand finale, the fireworks of diction exploding over the kitchen island, the flamboyant shock of the scandalous Cinnamon Toast Crunch announced with Madison Square Garden fervor.

My dad blasted Brahms and Gilbert and Sullivan in the mornings before school, jolting us awake with music for a coronation or village slaughter. As we were blinking into overalls over timpanis, "FIVE MINUTES!" was boomed after a bang at our doors, and dutifully I would respond, "Thank you five!" as he was the Zeusian stage manager in this the Olympian pageant of life.

My father's gravity yes could be terrifying to outsiders, but was mostly spectacular. Children operate at high stakes, and he met us there at every turn. (I am the oldest of three—Sam is three years younger, Harry eight.) When we were little, my dad played a particular game with us that if he hadn't trained us in tone and sense of occasion would have had us clambering to call 911. Playing the part of an innocent man reading to his children, he'd select a bedtime story for we T-rex-pajamaed fools. Cruelly he'd allow a few innocent minutes of harmless narration— an expert tactician. Then suddenly around page 3 he'd flinch, lowering *The Berenstain Bears* to his chest, now rising and falling with alarm.

". . . Did you guys hear that?"

He'd hold the silence for terrifying seconds, us straining to hear what it was.

"Nothing, nothing. I'm hearing things."

A few more pages. Then he snapped the book against his chest, clutching it like a cardboard rosary. This time, we saw in his face, the sound was unmistakable.

". . . Stay here. *Do not move.* Do you hear me?"

He'd then go downstairs to "check it out." Sam and I clutched each other telling ourselves we were just method-acting fear, but of course actually shaking with tears at the ready. We listened to him "search" the house, saying, "huh," calling up "probably just a false alarm," hearing him swing open the pantry ("Phew! Nothing here!") and creak open the washing machine ("Thank *GOD!*"). He yelled up to us:

"Must have been my imagination!" But then, horribly: ". . . I'll check the basement just to be safe."

The stairs to the bottom floor creaked with a concerned father merely protecting his children. We lay like child-sized ice picks rigid in bed, panting in terror at the line we knew was next; although the timing varied, sometimes it took ten minutes. Echoing up from two floors below us, we heard:

"Hello? . . . hello? . . . Oh my—DEAR . . . *GOD!!* What . . . What *are* you?!—I've never *seen* such—wait, please, my *children* are upstairs! Nn-no! . . . *AAAAAAUUUUUUGGGHHH!*"

. . . And then the horrifyingly specific sound effects of my father being *eaten*. By something we knew only as inhuman. And then silence. For a good three minutes. Just us breathing and holding each other, knowing what was coming.

And then. On the bottom basement stair.

STOMP.

We lose our minds screaming.

STOMP.

Choking screaming can't breathe.

. . . *STOMP.*

M-maybe it will just . . . leave? And we can call the police?

STOMPSTOMPSTOMPSTOMPSTOMP.

AAAAAAAAAHHHHHHHHH!

. . . . *STOMP.*

And then in a gravelly, terrifying, specific, and grounded British accent, a monster spoke to us.

". . . . . . *FEEEEE . . . FIIIIIIE . . . FOE . . . FUM.*"

We screamed like death was in the house and knew our names. The monster's monologue continued up the stairs and into the room, culminating of course with a guillotine of tickling by my father, now with removed glasses and a hallway hair ruffle for character work. But the stakes of the moment were never played for children. We were treated as worthy scene partners, screaming on cue, honored to be members of the cast. And, you know. A healthy demi-glace of PTSD to keep us honest.

If you are looking for a wisecracking chambermaid with crossed eyes and a secret, or an unstable trailer hermit with a limp who hears the future, or a skittish aunt who undercuts the queen with an aside about her ass size, or an Irish Jiminy Cricket making fart jokes at a funeral, consider my mother. Where my father is gravitas personified, my mother is 100 percent farce incarnate. At five two with orange-red hair and the map of Ireland on her face, she is a misbehaving sprite sticking her tongue out at me in the back row of my fifth-grade spelling bee. (The same bee where, when my opponent was given the word "crime" and I was given the harder "tomorrow," my mother mouthed to me, "BULL. SHIT.") As only the Irish can do, she had a tacit understanding that life was hard so why not laugh at how embarrassing every milestone was. She curated a trusty chest of costumes for us, collecting friends' regional theatre souvenirs for playdate fodder. I would wade in the pond for frogs in frayed understudy Eponine silks, eat raw batter in an already stained Lady Capulet cloak. When a German babysitter remarked that Americans had no sense of class regarding birthdays, my mother dressed us in wilted gowns and crumpled tails for sheet cake in the kitchen to ring in my ninth year.

When I was young, my mom and I were devoted fantasy scene partners. I read *Pride and Prejudice* aloud next to her bubble bath, her pretending to be the weary moneyed lady of the house and I her stumbly house-girl on a stool. We would stop an outdoor conversation if a bird got too close; the CIA, obviously. She once picked me up from sixth grade with her broken glasses duct-taped to her head, wandering the halls calling my name in an improvised song. She has recently taken to staging different Shakespearean tableaux with mini animal figurines on her pillow in the mornings, sending me pictures of a rubber ducky and ceramic rabbit doing the balcony scene on her duvet. I once watched her *heckle* her cleaning lady, standing near her saying ". . . faster, please . . . *God* you're bad at this." When I later pulled poor Patricia aside saying, "I hope you understand my mother's insane humor," Patricia looked at me like I was stupid. "Annie is magic."

My parents were so inherently their own miles-deep characters. I spent my childhood watching them disappear into others. The theatre was their office, and I came with them to work whenever it was allowed. I'm told that as an infant I was often passed through the ticket window to agreeable box office employees, squirming in their laps while my parents' iambic pentameter filtered through the PA. Later I was old enough to lie on the cot in their dressing rooms, listening to the same plays over and over again. I would memorize their cadence and lilts and pauses like math that got you drunk. If a stage manager was feeling the right mix of charitable and fuck it, they let me sit on their laps or curled on a crate to watch the show from the lighting booth. One such saint named Lloyd waved eight-year-old me into the booth every time I visited, let me call sound cues into the headset. He showed me how to push a lever that, when my TCBY-covered hand touched it, a warm orange light pierced the dark and filled my pinstriped dad's downstage face. After one performance late in the run, Lloyd whispered notes to me to give the actors. As instructed, I pulled aside the older actor in tweed and asked if he wouldn't mind picking up his cues in the garden scene. "John, we're adding two minutes that we can't afford."

My mom played Lincoln's sister-in-law at Lincoln Center, a fact I presented to my fellow second graders as a popularity jet-pack. I was met with blank stares. These stickerbook fucks didn't *get* it. I was spending weekends watching my mother hold court in a hoopskirt and a wig cap. If the secret-code knock came at her dressing room door, it was an ally in gossip—they were instructed to "come in and shut the door." They whispered scandals and elaborate musings while rouge and lashes were applied, transforming nineties moms into Civil War angels. My mom slipped me Werther's candies and put my name into the Secret Santa bowl, allowing me in the circle that felt like the most important society of elves that ever was.

She did a play out of town that involved a lot of newspaper snapping and tassels, one that I listened to over and over again from the ladies' shared dressing room. As if I controlled the weather myself, one night we were snowed in and couldn't drive back to the city. Mom left in her pin curls for the matinee the next day when we huddled together on the tiny dressing room cot for the night, flapper gowns hanging all around us like a fort. When I realized I had to cross the pitch-dark lobby to pee in the night, my mom murmured without looking up from her crossword, "Don't let the ghosts pinch your ankles."

She played a game with me where we'd decide on a secret signal, and she'd work it into her performance. A wig scratch in act 1 or a left-foot shake in the nightgown scene was her wink to me in the booth or random empty seat the ushers let me have last minute. Sometimes other actors played along, pointedly touching their nose or drawing out a part they knew I liked. Only now am I sure that there must have been a cohort of them flipping off the back of my head while I treated their church like camp. Imagining an eight-year-old giving me a note or waving at me from the mezzanine during a dramatic pause is raising my blood pressure in a way I'm not proud of.

Only when I was older did I start to understand the weight that my parents' superpower held. This little window to a world of magic meant you got to be kings and fairies and the funnest person in the room, dressing-room mates and hushed patrons leaning toward you in imagination communion. There's a beauty in letting your brain walk down a what-if road: *What if I were a murderer, what if I were a duchess, what if I dared, what if you and I.* Seeing the world and your own life as having a million different possibilities is a beautiful way to be—and to understand other people.

But I see now that it's also hard. It's hard to touch magic and then go home. It's hard to lift the rug of the world and see under it sparkling fantasy, then stand on that rug and make small talk about sconces.

The moments that I saw as the whole job I now see as the rare glints of yes that punctuate a lot of waiting and discomfort. And plain heartbreak. Not unlike being addicted to a drug that's always sold out. Watching plays now I'm so much more aware of the coughs of the audience, the loud candy wrappers during so-liloquies. A warning if we see a play together—as a patron, I am basically audience gestapo. I *will* whisper-scream at your mother if she thinks vibrate is silent. People are ripping their hearts open for less than an unemployment paycheck up there! How can you not see that your percussion bangle bracelets are robbing that downstage understudy of the one luxury in her life—thirty seconds of corseted ministry! I don't care if she's a bad actress! Her bio is tiny and this is her moment! Let her believe it's award winning! Oh God I just saw in her face that she can hear the hearing aid in row B; don't worry, angel, I'm going to motion to my husband to jab my program into the man's neck. Don't be a coward, honey, this monster has to be punished. Fine, I'll do it myself!

There was a play where my dad stood on the lawn of his family's house and did a monologue about why he left his wife and children, why he couldn't do it anymore. I was in the audience and ten. He said these words in a British accent, in clothes that weren't his. But I saw then that there were people in my father that I didn't know.

Then maybe, I thought, there are people in me, too. Maybe there's a bunch of them huddled up there in my weirdo mind. Maybe there are brainwomen.

I wondered what would make them happy. Oblivious then to the tattered empty seats spattering the house and the pain that one audience cough seared into you and the invisibility of the person tearing up next to that cough and the heartbreak of trading your crown for a diaper change and the embarrassment of being a jester with wings in a world rapidly outgrowing the need for them, in my standing ovation I thought, *this.*

4

GIRL BABY

As an elder Off-Broadway dressing-room mate once said to me between violent blush strokes, "There's no *good* time to gain fifty pounds, have your vagina rip open, and throw away eighteen years of your life."

It's August 2019. Suddenly I'm at that time in life where circumstance and body logistics have collided in the knifey corn maze of adulthood, and I'm now apparently going to try to have a baby. Which is certainly not the hand-over-heart teary *HURRAY* anthem I was hoping would pour out of my mouth at this twinkly milestone, but here we are. Charting the eyebrow patterns of my friends, I've realized that the lack of spice and magic in my voice on the subject is palpable, and I should probably stop offering it as lunch patter. When you treat a miracle like an errand, people don't love it.

Of course, the glue-filled wading pool of fear that my demons have soaked the topic of *motherhood* in feels superfluous. There are so many things that could go wrong that are out of my control. After two decades of hormonal birth control, maybe there's just an abandoned Samsung kiosk where my uterus should be, or I'll discover my partner has been killing Girl Scouts for years and I won't want his baby after all. Or, you know, the horrible thing could happen where it's there and then not there, and I'll be given a redundant ticket to Suicidal Junction and decide no more trying or sunlight. All these options truly terrify me because I am a person who never found a window of self-celebration and courage lasting enough to pierce my ears. If I miss the OK-let's-do-it-bus, it never comes again. Smooth earlobes and childless forever.

But more than my partner eating Thin-Mints-spleens, more than my eggs not understanding pilgrimage choreography on their own, more than depression mistaking a sigh for an entrance cue, I am afraid of this. I am afraid of going back to the internal cave where I'm supposed to have collected all the life lessons and weapons to arm my brain and present to a child, and I'll throw open the door, and it will be . . . empty. No captain's log of my own solidified identity, no menstrual-inked lab report of body knowledge, no stone-engraved tenants of Who I Am. Somehow, I have reached thirty-three ridden with disheartening tells that there might be nothing behind the curtain. And most of all, I'm terrified of having that particular kind of baby who will see this defect from the moment they open their eyes. I'm terrified of having a girl.

Growing up, I had the suspicion I had different brainwomen, yes. But what if everyone else was just pure id, *one* solidified person? What if I was just cycled selves existing for other people for who they needed me to be in that moment, and then alone I was just what, a Post-it? And if someone were to find that out and expose me? I guess I'd be executed, I breathed into my juice box and later a Shiraz.

I can't *have* a girl—she'd find out that my entire identity is based on hiding behind one.

At every phase of my life, I have had the complicated privilege—the life raft made of horsehair—of having a best girlfriend. They have mostly been a tiny bit older and a lot bit braver than me, marveling at their own bodies and instincts and thoughts, valuing their own story lines as something to water and explore. Early on I decided when it came to myself, such investment and inner curiosity would veer too close to vanity and risk, so was therefore out of the question. I couldn't believe my ludicrous fortune that I should be in the orbit of someone who had the code. I would look inward for the complex psyche I was apparently supposed to be cultivating and instead find a Claire's receipt and a now-moot, elaborate Playmobil soap plot. But certainly nothing that resembled a rabid eye inward, curious about my own cramps or clit. Thankfully the girl in the stroller or locker next to me always had this magical lair of self-wonder that she fed. That I would then copy.

I have spent my life lily-pad hopping from goddess to goddess, quietly plagiarizing their toe rings and credos, hoping that my mirroring would count as personhood, as if I were trying to get through Ellis Island with the "what she said" method. So much of my life was perched at the end of another girl's bed, in floral bike shorts or her hand-me-down Abercrombie do-you-know-where-your-children-are jeans, my body in full italics leaning toward her story and dreaming of the day I would morph into a protagonist in my own life.

Marie Black was the first. She was born two months after

me, upstairs. Our dads met at one of those colleges where when
someone says its name you scan the room for a shared eye roll,
like the dye you put in a pool for urine-shaming, but if there
was a fun version for friend-finding. Anyway, our dads probably bonded over being southern Episcopalians converting to
artistic New Yorkers, both a brand of Atticus Finch beat poet.
It was still the time when large swaths of Manhattan were un-
touched and going cheap, and they bought a building together in
one such ghost town on the East River. Bearded with tool belts,
they renovated it; a small former Gilded Age ice factory turned
abandoned-shadow-provider for the mob. Our building's mod-
est four-story frame stood huddled with other looming former
taverns of yore, smiling politely at each other across pee-soaked
cobblestone, wondering which would get them first, locusts or
gentrification. (There's now a Jamba Juice, so I guess . . . both.)
Our street hosted a bustling daily fish market, and had since before the Civil War. Probably the ye olde newsies caps and later
lapels of Pacino-y midnight dice-throwers and later still my
chocolate-stained preschool uniform all smelled like the same
trout-y hug. (As a result of this olfactory plague, it took me two
and a half decades to eat fish, when I wanted meeting a boy's family to go well so I force-swallowed chunks of salmon whole, like
Jager bombs.) Our ceiling was all beams, some strangely curved,
exposing their naval origin. Their wooden heft almost kissed my
top bunk, taunting me with the excruciating fact that my ceiling
was also Marie's floor, and that I'd have to wait a whole eight
hours to bound upstairs to see her again.

We were little, so the world hadn't taught us we were gross
yet. We spent our days like medieval kings in a war tent, existing
only to be merry and disgusting. The ghosts of mangled ice-factory

workers hopefully had some appreciation for alt-comedy, because we would rip our clothes off, perhaps diapers, and do the
Ace Ventura make-your-butt-talk thing but, um, with our own toddler vaginas—a searing memory I'm just going to have to live with
for the rest of my life. We also literally shat at the same time on the
same toilet, and then stood up and gendered the shits (this was a
different time) and then screamed goodbye as they sailed down the
toilet our stoned dads had installed a decade earlier. On paper we
were equal: both hyper cherubs of the generation where the old
money would run out, both chomping our Cheerios at the same
address, except I was inhaling mine at a medically unsafe speed
because I had to get upstairs to her, where the answers were.

There are mountains of pictures of us at the age when you
look like a little bald pink talent agent from the 1930s, and
you dig your seed-sized nails in someone's cheek to say hello, and
the anchovy of *doubt* couldn't possibly leak into your conscience
yet. But somehow my diapered brain made the distinction even
then; I knew nothing, and she knew everything. She was radi-
ant and wise, and my life's purpose was to study at her feet and
not fall out of her favor. Mind you, we were silly, tiny children.
Only later did I have the friendships where there was a deliberate
pressing down of spirit. This was something else.

If you're a girl, you know—some women just *have* it. And Marie
did. The way she poured food coloring in her yogurt with a lifted
brow and pursed mouth, letting the room know "I like things just
so," knowing from birth she wanted this and not that flavor of whatever life was offering. Even as a baby I noticed her little, snowy
pierogi shoulders were back with pride of self, relaxed with the
ease of already liking who she was—the rest was just decoration.

I was the opposite. In the same tutu bought at the same midtown quinceañera supply store, she looked like a sugarplum haiku where I looked like *Cuckoo's Nest* cosplay. I remember her looking in awe at her own finger painting, seeing O'Keeffe where I at first saw Grover vomit but then immediately understood it to be O'Keeffe. Even in size-four Keds she was running her life as a conscious location scout for the Oscar biopic, christening some Popsicle flavors and playground associates in the *yes* column and banishing with precision the unfavorables to the *no*. Sensing no internal judges' panel of my own, I just stood near hers and nodded.

Quickly, I realized that a girl's life has many show-your-work moments—a preschool barrette choice, a sticker here, a lanyard there—a calculated nod toward the solidified person you were. Growing up, I watched the boys around me living as if every moment was a gap year free-write, while for the girls it was a perpetual conclusion paragraph on the completed identity you were submitting for inspection at every new milestone. If boyhood was mosh-pitting with a knife through a buffet of experiences, girlhood was a Build-A-Bear Workshop in 1609.

In this protected biodome of time where youth was still just learning not to shit your pants, I was able to rehearse a self that three decades later a menthol-smoking therapist suggested was unhealthy. (Neither are Newports, Susan!) Instead of seeing my own life as a pulsing, empty scroll to fill with identity, I saw it was safer to just exist as a fan museum of hers. I would wait for Marie to choose a color headband, then test the waters if this was an instance where choosing the same color would be a symbol of allegiance or blasphemy. In some pictures we are matching *Shining* twins; in others I am consciously bridesmaiding—the same, but just . . . less.

———

There is one picture that says it all. My mother sewed and hers did not, a calculation I foolishly did not take into consideration leading up to our fifth Halloween. The day we met in our shared hallway to trick-or-treat was a kindergarten *et tu* moment felt round the world. I walked out in a beautifully appointed, pink, full princess fairy tableau, a real nod to my mother's sense of theatrics and detail. All her years of gossiping in costume shops had led to her making her feral five-year-old shine on Halloween. Usually I was a stained human jungle, but for some reason we really Martha Stewart Bibbidi-Bobbidi-Booed this holiday. There was a collective "oo" vowel when I floated into the hall—although the two sets of parents were playing separate intentions with their vowels. From mine it was two actors sensing the genre and adding to the wonder bubble of a moment with a sighed "my goodness." For Marie's parents it was . . . fear. For they knew what was behind door number two. It swung open with a crashing bang, the sunlight blinding all of us as we screamed. (It was at night and not near a window, thereby impossible, but this is how it is in my memory, no notes, please.) My liege, my goddess on high, my Jim Jones as Baby Jane, stepped into the hallway. If there was a stage manager calling sound cues in heaven, the lilting, whistley sound in a spaghetti Western face-off would have been speakered from the sky.

Referencing the picture of this moment while at home on a recent Christmas, I referred to Marie's costume as a rabbit. My mother corrected me in a tone as if we were in Hogwarts and I had summoned a certain name.

"She was a *dog,* Betty."

"But . . . the rabbit ears . . ."

"Are you insane? She. Said. She. Was. A. Dog."

And the matter was dropped, because now I remembered.

Departing from her usual float-walk, Marie jerk-waddled into our hallway. A furry bath mat was stapled around her body, rendering her immobile and insane. She had an Easter Bunny headband that—we soon learned in high-risk, real-time education—was dog's ears. She looked like an extra in *Oliver!* if the production were set in a Sasquatch dementia ward. Already enraged with displeasure at her own masquerade and needing her court to perpetuate a whisper campaign that she was a Westminster finalist, she turned to take in my garment.

"I like your costume."

Marie's words hung in the air like buffering emojis—were they hearts and thumbs or were they knives and poops? We didn't know. My stomach and organs do-si-do-ed. I knew it was my turn to speak.

"I *love* your costume."

I could feel my mother's eyes on me. She knew what I wanted to do more than anything. I wanted to trade. Into my glittered temple she beamed the sentence "Offer to trade, and you will never taste chocolate again."

But in retrospect I know she understood. The jester gene is hereditary. The jester is not supposed to out-queen the queen. It was the first moment where I felt sick in taking up too much space, where on the other side of the door I had twirled and screamed. Copying her mannerisms and playing the goblin to her damsel was much, much easier than the night I had as the winner of Halloween. I hated it. I over-pigeon-toed my rainboots under the pink tulle—swaying in little wobbling *sorry*s to stay beta.

You know where you stand when you're the lackey. You know your lines; you know the scene's turns. You zing compliments, one-liners, the occasional tap dance, but then you scurry to the safety of the wings. There in the dark, in a wig cap and a hoop skirt, you can watch the *star* do all the scary stuff. That night I must have offered Marie everything I had in candy-trade to erase my off-script sparkle. November 1's garbage saw rain-soaked fairy wings and a pail full of Mounds.

Where I had assumed there were no set-in-stone rules self-chiseling in my soul, there was apparently one. A rule I'm embarrassed to say lasted thirty years. The failure of shining is too great a risk. Let the shinier do it first, and see if they die trying.

Our family moved away from New York and our cartoons and Campbell's den when I was nine, a decision that felt like my parents were informing me we'd be throwing my legs in a wood chipper and tossing the remaining stub on a cruise to Alcatraz. Whatever piddly roots of who I was were still clinging to Marie's steroidal oak self. If extricated, I would die. But we got in the Volvo and moved to Connecticut. Marie waved from her cereal. I threw myself against the car window and sobbed.

Of course, to say I had no identity was a lie I was telling myself. Instead I was very much exactly me: a marinara-stained character actress, screaming at the sky and lifting a brow every third sentence. But I had already cast said character as a foil in someone else's story. I worried that alone, I didn't exist. I needed Marie. Our pen pal letters were heartsick and illustrated, often in character as Civil War sisters who had been separated because of disease. Marie once enclosed a tea-stained, crumpled-for-effect healing recipe, as I had been sent to the country for yellow fever. I replied with a shakily written (being near dead) note on a torn hymnal page, begging for her prayers and salves, fearing I wouldn't see morning. But this wasn't enough to sustain us, and slowly she shifted from OshKosh Messiah to erstwhile sensei. Floating in space grasping at meaning with no alpha-she for a compass, I eventually found Bunny.

In middle school, Bunny Scott fished her mother's stolen Virginia Slims out of our trusty hollow log in the woods and leaned her head back like she had a contract with MGM as she told me about how when she and Zach from camp hooked up he had made her squirt. Since I had barely kissed someone, I made a quiet internal note to self-guillotine at my earliest convenience. I met Bunny when I transferred from the former one-room schoolhouse to the everyone-is-a-miracle-homework-is-optional establishment. Here children wandered the halls without shoes or laws, calling teachers by their first names and using a poet's soul as a pass to put tacks in Mark R's Fritos. Having spent her childhood at both said school and her own school of personal yes, Bunny was light-years ahead of me at every daring milestone. Legends of her elusive watercolored fuckfest of an art camp were the envy of our class, each autumn bringing tales of how far behind I'd fallen while she squirted ahead. She was *gorgeous,* duh, a preteen Charlize in ripped-on-purpose overalls and light-up Doc Martens. She did all the things I thought you weren't allowed to do— chop all your hair off, think Jonah's dad was hot, read novels for fun. (Being old enough now to have the fashion mistakes of my pubescence be vintage-irony-wear for current pop stars, I smile at how every Skechers-and-lollipopped influencer is plagiarizing 1998 Bunny.)

Every girl has a corruption doula of a friend at that age, guiding you swiftly into making your mother stop sleeping. Bunny gave me *The Bell Jar* and Fiona Apple and her mother's Marlboro Reds, an insane cigarette for a twelve-year-old, like huffing a 1923 dugout. But we'd smoke five in a row deep in the woods behind her house, her house that was so much cooler than mine, even the trees in her woods more chic and over it than my parents' desperate no-chill maples. I hid her copy of *Lolita* inside the hymnal binder in the choir loft during church, desperately trying to create tragic stakes to report to her. Since I had the physique of a malnourished Peter Pan understudy, she'd graciously allow me to scavenge through her Goodwill pile. Eventually my wardrobe existed almost exclusively of sexualized skater clothes she had sauntered in two years ago and now hated. The Gift of the Fucking Magi came when she deemed me worthy of her jeans that she'd cut in half and joined back together with a trillion safety pins. Walking into circle time wearing them with a LITTLE PRINCESS? ROYAL *PAIN* T-shirt, I felt like Keith Richards holding a sedated tiger. But I could not shake the flash on Alessia B's face when she saw me. I told myself it was envy. But the sweetness in her voice at what came next took care of me in a way that hurt more than a slap would have. It was a twelve-year-old's pity. When our retired psychic of a teacher used her indoor voice to compliment my pants, Alessia breathed to the floor, ". . . they're Bunny's." But I guess, so was I.

With Bunny I workshopped a role I would reprise elsewhere again and again, Igor to her Queen Frostine. While I certainly cracked jokes and sang my assigned *Moulin Rouge!* role in our duets, we fell comfortably into a sort of star and assistant dynamic. Now as an actor sometimes around fancier actors who have people they love who are also on the payroll, I wince with the realization that the absence of "And how are *you?*" is a job. I could have been contributing to my 401(k) since Elmo-dom. When I ended the friendship years later on a phone call during which I pulled up the entire northwest-corner fibers of my bedroom rug, I was monotone. I needed to end the dynamic that I thought she alone engineered.

I was wrong. To paint myself as the perpetual shackled hamster to her Veruca Priestly is not factual. It's a nice story I've told myself to get the coveted eight hours of nocturnal world-escape. Bunny didn't write the rules alone. What *is* true is that together we established a dynamic where I knew her boyfriends' astrological signs and everything that ever happened to her three times over, while my own life and thoughts were regarded as a sort of 1850s gay uncle's, avoided like spinach in the teeth of a stranger. We spent five, six nights a week together for years—my bony colonial kid-ghost body knotted at the floral couch next to her bed, drunk from screwdrivers we insisted hit the spot. The couch was under a poster of *Slums of Beverly Hills,* and I shrank away from Natasha Lyonne's what-the-fuck-are-you-doing glare. Meeting Lyonne a decade later, I had to remind myself that her posters were not preteen liar-spies and hadn't reported my shame tally to her in advance of our sharing a cigarette on Forty-seventh Street. Still, I shrunk when we shook hands.

True, Bunny didn't listen and was never going to win a curiosity prize. But this is also because I insisted. She was the puppeteer, but I had a vulnerability taser in my pocket, making sure she pulled the strings so I'd never have to answer questions about who I was. Because I didn't know. Or hated what little I did. Being near someone who never stops to check in if they've told this story before or if their friend is choking means you never have to take the mortifying risk of being a person out loud. I was her spaghetti-strapped lackey for sure. But she was my tube-topped guinea pig. I would crack wise and dole compliments from the trenches, then cower watching her twirl and flail through the actual battlefield. Only when I saw she didn't die from flirting or thinking did I skulk out and perform a spineless forgery.

Our love died in the city devoted to it. We went to Paris with my family, a halting change in our dynamic, as I was always the guest and preferred to be dropped off at the bottom of my drive-way. We were at separate schools by now, and Bunny didn't know or understand, but I was drowning in sad at mine. She also didn't ask. We snaked through Paris hiding from my family while she did not ask. I fumed to the pavement. It was the summer when Paris was a billion degrees of glue soup, and sweat spilled blue mascara down our faces as we tried and couldn't keep the marriage alive. She was detailing a hookup story I'd heard twice before. In unison with Bunny's lilt, I breathed the story's punch line: "He sat on the fucking Furby." She looked up at me, hurt, doe-eyed, like I'd punched her birthday cake.

I'm dying, I should have said. *I'm not taking care of myself. I'm afraid of this blackness lacing my days. I need you to listen to me and probably a hug.* Instead I threw my cigarette in the Seine. Months later, calling her from that rug felt one-sided and righteous, but only now I see my idiocy. I was seventeen, and every system I'd built to protect myself was only to hide, and in a vacuum I treated myself like I didn't exist. I'd stopped eating and stopped getting out of bed. How could I be angry at the people I trained to never look behind the curtain to do exactly as I asked.

There were other women after her—a girl in high school whose books I literally carried and later (after her expulsion) whose ex-boyfriend I let frantically sign the alphabet in my underwear in a pitiful attempt at justice. And others. Even now quiet demons in me seek out dynamics where I plagiarize bravery and rope off accountability. But my friends now have my number to a mortifying degree and don't allow such cowardice. I still worry that a lifetime of treating women like boxcars to run alongside and hide in has left me being-less.

There was an uncomfortable period where I had to interact regularly with a boss's daughter. She was my worst nightmare. Her smile plummeted to Hades into a Maggie Smith frown when I entered a room. Shifting her usual twinkle, she stared through me with dead eyes, bathing in disappointment. It felt like we were perpetually at my law school graduation, where only *she* knew I had forged my LSATs and was obligingly raising a glass as she waited to press send on an exposé. That's how she looked at me. Every day. One dark evening I was seated next to her at a dinner party, where our conversation sent me speed-trotting to the bathroom, swallowing tears. Twice. In the cab home, I sobbed to my boyfriend that she was, pure and simple, "an asshole." She was two years old.

In the same Christmas nostalgia session as the famed Halloween dog photo, my mother selected a Polaroid of toddler me. I'm diapered and plotting, my dumpling body twisting one way and my face squinting back, scheming.

"That which hath made me drunk hath made me bold," my

mother expertly captioned. A long silence and then, "You were terrifying."

I looked at her like she had revealed my adoption.

"What?"

My mother looked at me like I was denying war crimes.

"You always had it all figured out. We were afraid of you."

I opened then shut my mouth to combat this erasure. I thought of my boss's daughter, how much insane projection I radiated at this literal *baby*. I replayed all the moments where to baby boys I squealed, "Say cheese!" and to baby girls I pursed, "Well *she* certainly loves the camera." I thought of Marie. Now purple-haired and literary across the continent, I wonder what her take on our nursery era would be. I know a Birkenstocked Bunny remembers a different story than I do. Bunny had pain I couldn't see either. Fifteen years after Paris, I walked the half mile between our apartments to see her. Pregnant and sunburned, Bunny told me I was the only person who'd ever broken her heart.

Many of the friendships I have now that keep me from driving into the sea started with an afar eye roll, then the later shock of sharing hate of self and love of farce. I am frustrated that I have to keep learning this lesson over and over, assigning each new scarf wearer to the aloof perfection category, wasting so much time before realizing sameness.

But alongside this poison where we silently cast each other as the enemies is the good part. While we are quietly afraid of each other, women are also braiding identities as we pass, huddled together in phases until you outgrow each other. Maybe existing as a counterfeit collage of every woman I've known is not an anomaly, but just how it works. You wash your hair how she did, ask for a raise how she did, flick the lighter how she did, hog the covers, kiss the boy, ask the question, walk shrugging into the darkness. I wonder if my bun approach could be traced back to a medieval sleepover. Looking back and seeing the loose threads of the girls I worshipped as impeccable, I am sad. I hope I have the bravery to smile into the face of a daughter, and ask her questions.

5

ADVICE TO A YOUNG ACTRESS

Congratulations, young lady! Through a humbling cocktail of luck, groveling, and the troubling brain problem that enables you to emote for money, you are going to be an *actress*. Maybe you have just graduated from a theatre program where you mostly sobbed about your childhood in a teal movement pant for four years. You are known on campus for your moving performance in an all-vowel-no-consonants *Antigone,* but about corporations. As a kid, you belted *Guys and Dolls* into a shampoo-mic with your cousins, giving them harsh but necessary notes when they butchered your choreography for the big Easter performance that no one asked for. Later you morphed from vaudeville ham to turtlenecked depressive, your journal an addled Edgar Allan Bradshaw run-on sentence, desperate for the day when you could channel your darkness into a role and not a bad poem. Your girlhood has been your Mr. Miyagi training for your career—your jazz hands at bath time the wax-on for your Tony, your sobbing to the middle school mirror the wax-off for your Oscar. And now, finally, you're an actress. All you have to do is claim your trophies.

Uh-huh.

Just a couple quick thoughts before you're out the door to your first audition. Lucky for you, this is a different time from when this here old show pony was first out of school. Back in 2008, the entertainment industry hadn't been guilted into performed feminism yet. Ten years ago, the misogyny requirements were in bold at the top of the email. Now they're a size-two footnote under a Greta Thunberg GIF. Back then we knew outright that auditioning as an actress meant be hot and heartbreaking impossibly at once. Tap-dance in a transparent smock and beret, tears gushing out of one eye while the other winks for sexual whimsy.

You were allowed to try for Lip-Biting Binder Holder for about two years, until quickly graduating to Arms-Folded Sweater Woman. The audition scenes were the same: scene 1, talk fast to prove brain; scene 2, talk low to prove sexy; scene 3, talk through sobs to prove unstable. Inevitably, a rapey gargoyle in stained cashmere pajamas would graze your areolas with his elbow and thereby deem you worthy of playing Waiter With Question.

But it's different now!

. . . Eh, kinda.

Now the secret's out that we have organs and ambitions, and the world is slowly starting to adjust. We are now in a strange Frankenstein time where we're trying to sell the merch of a feminist victory before having the victory itself. Being an actress now feels like a bizarre hybrid of 1952 and 2053. It's nodding *yes, everything's fixed,* on a "Women: We Did It!" panel while spending all of your still-smaller-than-the-boys' paycheck on sheep-semen lotion to beg the world to believe you're still twenty-three. It seems that as we are winning the war of getting some fart jokes and producer credits, just as quickly rise the smoke and mirrors demands. We are being handed the keys to the city, but with a contour brush attachment. When I hold a microphone and say things like "Now more than ever," I mean it, but I'm simultaneously disguised as the porniest Saint Bart's poodle version of myself. I'm usually wearing high heels, shoes designed to put calf muscles into a mini seizure so that one might entice a landowner to trade a wife for goats. My face is contoured—a makeup method the straight community has appropriated from drag queens. My lips are lined five inches from the actual mouth part, and my cheeks have a space bar of soil painted below them. Without this Houdini trickery, I now feel I am disgusting. We are told two opposing things: put on a blazer and scream fuck into a mug, but also arch your back for a selfie and whisper thanks into a teacup.

The first big TV job I auditioned for, I was told that getting naked on camera was the necessary toll to pay if I wanted the part. With tears in my eyes, I told them that I didn't play Hamlet in 2003 only to be a blow-up doll for hire who thinks iambic pentameter is an STD. I put my things in a briefcase, looked around the room one last time, and, to the shock of the producers, I left the audition. On the drive home I scream-sang Springsteen and pounded the steering wheel, just my grandmother's granddaughter, with the GPS programmed for nowhere at all.

Just kidding. I immediately took off all my clothes and also asked if I should take out the recycling 'cause it looked full. They were like, "Um, ma'am, we'll let you know when the sex scene is scheduled. For now please put on a flannel and call your parents." (Looney Tunes Snark Rosetta Stone: I got the part and said, "Yes, thank you, I will show my boobs. See you at work.") Because I wanted this job. I had spent eight years crying and dying on one-off episodes of *Police Hospital Diaper City* and screeching through Off-Off-Broadway plays for three Upper East Side corpses and no one else. My bank account was an empty parking garage with one dead horse. Then my inbox dinged with this dream job. Good writing, good actors, good paycheck, in New York. The albino shooting star unicorn on a leap year.

Behind the casting table, there were a handful of men and a handful of women. I had a feeling if I could convince the boys I checked the Bratz doll boxes, and secretly convince the women there was a wart-covered character actress trapped inside said doll, I could do the impossible. I could finally slip through the door to the elusive actor Eden: getting to do the thing you love more than anything for a real living.

The job itself, while a dream come true, was a constant frantic tap dance between the two gendered peanut galleries. One was a khaki-ed platoon of elder bros, one a cat-hair-cardiganed gaggle of she-geeks. The women sect consisted of the cerebral former playwrights who wrote for the show and the intimidating female Pacinos who starred on it. The bros were new, recruited in this later season to spike viewership, and their pitch was *more areolas.* ENTER GILPIN.

The way I felt on this job was the way I felt much of my career, and still do even now that Gloria Steinem is on tote bags. It's like the scene in *Mrs. Doubtfire* where Robin Williams sprints back and forth to the restaurant bathroom, frantically changing from clowny dad to angelic drag grandma, trying impossibly to be both at once. I had to assure the khaki bros I was centerfold-y enough while trying to convince the she-cardigans I knew who Samuel Beckett was.

For four seasons, it had been a brilliant show about no-frills, complicated women who were good at their jobs. Pony-tails, ChapStick, and gravitas. Then in season 5 I came in to play a sex-crazed ditz who wore stilettos to work and could barely put a subject and predicate together. I was made to look like Dolly Parton if she ruled a corporation in space. While my costars wore sweatpants and hoodies, I was shrink-wrapped in hot pink mouse napkins. I had (expertly done) *Dynasty*-level hair and makeup, teals and purples and glitter carving a Disney sex wench out of my pilgrim face. I played a doctor. My costume for my first scene was a piece of tape. (Yes, really. This I'm sure has my Catholic ancestors on a permanent rotisserie grave-spin.) Body shame and awareness flooded back into my psyche like a toxic brain enema. I told myself that if I could secretly lace some mental illness and farce in the character, I would be able to sleep.

I knew the odds. Ten trillion actresses in the world, a handful of tiny fleeting opportunities that may never come again. I had to make this work. Between sex scenes, I'd try to shoehorn in some Blanche DuBois. I'd quietly pepper some Monty Python into her strut. Instead of a witless bimbo, I tried to play a lazy dame, bored and insane instead of incapable and simple. Slowly the women writers sent subliminal messages to me that they were receiving my secret transmissions. Instead of the character's original "likes" and "ums," they peppered in wild-eyed theories and thousand-yard-stare non sequiturs. As long as I pressed my taint against the lens every few episodes, the bros didn't seem to care if I made weird faces. I made friends with the legends who were my female scene partners. I threw myself under the bus at every pos-sible between-takes opportunity to try to convince them I was not a selfie-taking art killer but a shadow-loving carnie person, *just like them.* On days where I had dream-come-true scenes with actresses I had quietly worshipped from the couch for years, I came to work with a journal full of ideas and risks. The other days were less fun, when it was time to mime a blow job or walk slowly across a room taking off my beautifully tailored costume. Those days I came to work with an empty stomach. But this, apparently, was the toll for the dream.

Although it wasn't as obviously black-and-white as this particular job, this is the contradiction tango I have danced for most of my career. And you, future actress, you will, too. From audition to talk show and everything in between.

The Audition: Be Both Her and Her but Definitely Not You

In an audition, often the first round is just you and, more times than not, a female casting director. She puts you on tape. That tape is then sent to, more times than not, a room full of men. (Or at least these were the usual demographics until recently.) The problem is, what wins *her* favor in wanting you for a part is different from what wins *his*. Or perhaps more fairly, what a "creative" wants in an actress versus what a producer wants. And they often contradict. It's your job then, impossibly, to attempt both at once.

We are all in this business in part to enact some sort of high school revenge tableau. (A therapy aside: mine is making a career out of playing the Bunnys and Hadleys to prove to my ribby former self the silence wasn't all for naught. YIKES!) It is the actress's job to convince you she is both the headgear-wearing, overlooked wallflower whom you can finally grant time in the sun *and* the sparkling flawless cheerleader you can finally control. You have to be both. The current trend of posting a soft-core sel-fie with a self-deprecating caption is the perfect encapsulation; *I am perfect, but I promise, I have no idea.*

Here's a how-to guide to attempt to fulfill this impossibility.

Let's say you're auditioning for the lead role of Chloe. What are you going to wear? No, not your old teal movement pant. How will you prepare? No, not charting Chloe's family tree in blood. You cannot megaphone that you are an actor.

You gotta apology-whisper that you're . . . *Chloe.* You've just existed forever as Chloe. Wear tight clothes to show your mea-surements, but a baggy (open) sweater over it to show you have trauma and hate your measurements. Wear a lot of makeup to apologize for having an alive face, but not so much that people think you're a rabid narcissist who likes their own alive face. As you are is disgusting, dolled up is unlikable. Find the middle. Tug at your sleeves in self-hate for the first scene, then scratch an itch on your back in the second so the sweater rides up, accidentally showing the spoils of the spin class you sobbed through. Uh-oh, we're veering toward unlikable again, so make a self-deprecating joke between the first and second scenes. This way while you're featuring that you'll look great in the blow job ukulele montage, you're *also* saying *Look, I might kill myself at any second.* And that? Is adorable.

The Meeting: Shiny and Abs or Gritty and Poem

In recent years I have experienced the confounding next level of casting, where there is no audition, but a *meeting*. It is a ritual I do not understand. If you were to hire a crane operator, would you hold interviews at a Blue Bottle to see which construction worker had the sexiest anecdote about their quote tattoo? No. You'd end up hiring an unstable bassist whom you didn't know needs LASIK, mowing down pedestrians with a machine he's never touched. This is how we get bad accents and fake crying in film, children. 'Cause someone was humble in cashmere and told a good Burning Man story over tuna rolls, and no one said, "But just checking, can you act?" #Abolishthemeeting

It will, of course, not be abolished, because though we are past *certain* aspects of troubling lunches, the entertainment business is still fueled by them. Even post–Me Too it's still a date of sorts, maybe with less thigh-pawing. Even when someone's not trying to fuck you, a meeting is still Mind Game Jenga. Let's play!

You have to spend the first ten minutes guessing which version of a woman they think you are, then convince them that no, no, you are the other. When you arrive at the meeting, rapidly assess your matcha partner. Are they a crabby genius in a hat who makes a show of rolling their eyes at the menu font? OK, chances are he wants a French aerialist who thinks acting is stupid for the role and not you. In their eyes, you are a cheesy choice. You will ruin their art. Your eyeliner and posture and easy laugh are all evidence that you're the vapid perfume cloud that ignored them in high school. Your job is now to spend this meeting convincing this person that that girl ignored *you,* too. That you hate yourself. That your life has been full of darkness. Sunlight? The VMAs? I don't even know what those things are. I'm damaged, I'm broken. (An exercise in Marketing the Salem.) Mention every book you've ever read. Allude to maybe being a genius, but in a way where you're a lost (French!) vessel who doesn't even *know* it— but of course not smarter than them. You need them. Alone you are floating in space with all this pain but with *their* vision? You could finally channel it all into their script. Which like, *really* spoke to you by the way. It (hand over heart) I mean (shake head) . . . (close eyes and pause) . . . and honestly you can just kind of leave it there. They want to be complimented but will be offended by specifics.

There is the opposite kind of meeting, of course, so be prepared for that, too. There is nothing like the feeling of waving hi to your meeting companion and seeing immediately in their eyes that you're not shiny enough. I have "met" with big scary people who were casting movies where they want women with purple eyes and no bowels. Movies that would turn pretentious college you's stomach, the McDonald's of films, but that would put you on billboards and buy your mom a house. Where even though the role is an abused gas station attendant in a town with no vegetables, you have to look like you've never not been to the gym and have only known greens. That when you turn your head, your neck skin doesn't fold. That you have a self-taser installed in your tailbone that goes off when you furrow your brow or use four-syllable words, so you never do.

In *these* meetings, it's your job to convince them that yes, I *am* that vapid perfume cloud. But now she's not ignoring you in Bio, she's here, needing *you*. Convince them that through you, they can go back in time and *stop* that girl in the hallway. And put her in a crate. There, they can tell her things like "You're welcome" and "Only *he* can improvise."

If it's *this* kind of meeting, get there early to choose the seat with less sunlight so it doesn't hit your face on the side where you have a big zit. Or reveal that you're over seventeen. (Honestly, do this for both meetings. The auteur doesn't want their French muse to have crow's feet either.) Still tell a story about hating yourself, but make it fun and keep it short. Say the word "badass" a lot—it's a fun buzzword that makes everyone feel like they're checking feminism boxes, but really it just means *Don't worry, I have good triceps.* Triceps that in a vacuum are just floating in space and tan, but with *your* vision? I could finally channel my triceps into a script. Which like . . . *really* spoke to me, by the way. It's (hand over heart) *badass*!

There was a day where I had these two types of meetings back-to-back. The first was to play a "bookish, scrawny, troubled butch lesbian coder" in a gritty television show. On walking up to the jean-jacketed, braless writer, it was immediately clear that she had written the character based on herself. She was the epitome of cool. Within thirty seconds, it was further clear to me that she'd been forced to take our meeting and thought I was all wrong. I was wearing a tight black shirt, and she squinted at my body like she was trying to read a gross inscription. She greeted me with "Oy *vey*, your *body*, you're like, 'Oh, hi.'" She mimed me entering the room, I guess with a body, while shrugging a sort of ditsy "What? I don't get it." A brand of compliment that only exists woman to woman—one soaked in disdain disguised as self-deprecation. A sort of *must be nice having lived your whole life getting out of jury duty by twirling your hair, the rest of us have been over here reading Kant and laughing at you.* So, of course, I spent the meeting trying to convince her I had a library card and PTSD. I dished out traumatic stories like they were Bagel Bites I brought to throw at a zoo lion to please it. I acrobatted *Gatsby* puns into a story where I was the butt of every joke. SAT words and self-hate were my best bet to win this meeting. By the end we had both cried, and for a few strange minutes it felt like we were going to kiss, which was a twist. Now that we were soul mates, she offered to drive me to my next meeting. She put on a mix and lit a menthol. I closed my eyes pretending the unfamiliar song conjured a devastating memory.

The next meeting was at a studio where you basically have to give four pee samples to be allowed inside. There is intensely elaborate security for the kingdom of golf-carting, cashmere travel mugs that run Los Angeles. I was late. Late, because I had spent the morning convincing the Dylan-esque writer that I was a tobacco-y haiku. It would have been brand-suicide to do something as high-strung as check the time. Exiting her Volvo at the studio gates I . . . I *saluted* goodbye to my . . . new girlfriend? An actual salute, as if it were something I did regularly as a misunderstood poet person. I sauntered away until she was out of sight. Then I started sprinting. I ran the addled hamster route the guard had drawn me on the studio map, remembering now that my agent had emphasized what a big get this meeting was and that they had limited time.

The assistant's face fell when I asked for the bathroom, seeing in her eyes that she was trying to communicate *but they're already pissed*. I know, Kelsey, but fifteen minutes late with more eye-shadow is better than ten minutes late looking like myself. We both know that.

The Bluetoothed woman didn't look up when I was shown in with my plastic water bottle the size of a Ping-Pong ball. She was typing furiously and sighing. I sat posing in a few minutes of wordless keyboard clacking that I knew was punishment for my tardiness, a sort of reclaiming the power of whose time was less important to whom. "OK, hi," she eventually offered. She rubbed her eyes. She looked at me for four seconds and then refocused her eyes to the correct focal point—the middle distance between us where she could think about who might be *actually* right for this job. And lunch.

Whereas I had spent my morning trying to convince a wallflower vagabond system-fucker that I was one, too, I knew my afternoon's job was to insist the opposite. That I'm a vanilla, hollowed-out Christmas ornament. I'm a gleaming mirror, reflecting whatever you want. I *am* the perfume cloud. I am a difficult but brief fort-night away from chiseled abs, I promise. The eighties? Not sure what you mean. I was born under Bush II. What is this irrelevant heavy square pile on your coffee table? Books? I like juice. I like crying on stationary bikes. I'm badass! Sorry, that was too loud. I'm badass. Sorry for being late, it's 'cause of dumb. Dumb no his-tory can be whatever vacant jean shorts gun holder part this is. Tan. Cheekbone. Was made to stand in front of a green screen agreeing with dude. Was never part of dream but world tells me this job would fix sad.

I was too shiny this morning but now nowhere near enough. She interrupted every answer with another question, sprinting through it like we're running lines for the script of the slower kinder meeting we'll have later, but we of course will not, and suddenly I'm in the hall again and . . . OK I'm crying, that's disappointing. I veer to the bathroom. On the toilet my mind offers a self-pity retrospective montage, replaying the day's *oof*. I zone out and put a new toilet paper roll in the empty dispenser painted the colors of the franchise that bought Bluetoothwoman her third Lexus. I realize what I'm doing. I hate myself for completing a chore here that feels insurmountable in my own home. In an act of if-a-tree-falls defiance, I put the toilet paper back on the shelf. I look in the mirror. I try a smile. I have a leaf in my teeth. A leaf I'd eaten before both meetings. I'd given my body a leaf then spent the day throwing it under the bus.

I didn't get either part.

So anyway this is what you do, OK?! It's easy. There's a little *but wait* voice in you that will be annoying, but it gets quieter. Soon you'll barely hear it, and treating your identity like a Swiss Army knife of traits to perform and muffle will be as easy as lying to yourself. Sorry, as easy as sleeping. Night night.

In the last week of the last season of the trade-nudity-for-nuance job, I let myself cheat a little. It had been three years of devoting a large part of my brain and day to making sure I looked like the least gelatinous Playmate I could be. Three years of 5:00 a.m. exercise classes before work, the kind where Soviet chipmunk women screamed into a headset that your dysmorphia was actually codified law. If I had spent that time sleeping another hour, I would have been better at my job. For three years, I avoided any foods that would make a viewer think I lived in the world, foods that would have given me better energy to do the scenes *after* the soft-core interludes. If I had just had the hamburger, I would have been better at my job. Three years of avoiding eye contact with the dudes writing these pants-plummeting scenes, when maybe one uncomfortable conversation could have stopped them. If I had been a little braver, I would have been better at my job.

I'm not entirely blaming myself. I just mean . . . it is going to take centuries to stop the chorus of people telling you that your highest purpose as a woman is to minimize your waistline and being. Your realizing that that's bullshit before they do will just be more efficient.

(She said to the mirror.)

The night before my very last day of filming this show, I had a culinary one-night stand. I ate a lamb curry and flourless chocolate cake and whiskey, the Holy Trinity of Not Allowed. But I was finally done with the naked scenes—all that remained was a long day of emoting in the background in a lab coat. The final morning I sat in the makeup chair for one last two-hour car wash of disguise. Mink lashes were glued to the eyelids that twenty years before I wiped fake tears from in a sandbox, pretending in OshKosh that I was Barbara Stanwyck in distress. I tried to keep my head as still as possible as my hair was teased into something so far from the limp brown strings I'd once tucked into a skull-cap to play Tiny Tim. I felt sick thinking that achieving my dream meant being cruel to myself along the way. That visibility meant invisibility.

I also felt sick because I . . . felt . . . sick. My stomach suddenly started making noises like a colossal demon waking up hungover in a cave it doesn't recognize. This demon started to turn over. Suddenly the dynamics of digestion were a tidal wave that I could not control.

Something within me was angry.

You forgot me. You pushed me down. You treated me unfairly. You forgot that the ugly is what got you here, the rare thing you like about yourself. You sold me and ran from me. And now, I'm back, shaking you and screaming that you can't kill me, don't you dare.

I walked into the hallway and shat my pants.

6

AWAY

The second I got tits I also got eyes that rolled and arms that crossed. But before then, at thirteen, I passed for a child. A boy child. Once on a field trip to Ellis Island a girl in tears asked me for a picture, mistaking me for the youngest Hanson brother. This is just to say, when I was little, I was *little*. Thinking of that person now with their bucket-hatted head against the minivan window on the way to *boarding school* feels insane. I was small and strange, and could not wait to further the feeling of having my door locked at all times by applying to a high school where I'd also sleep. Where all my experiences could be a secret, monitored by well-meaning clipboarded maxi skirts, but a secret.

Bunny and I had spent eighth grade spilling nail polish on brochures of all the same sleepaway magic-less Hogwarts, rabid to be hours away from our Samantha dolls. Out loud to Bunny's ceiling, I insisted it was because I also couldn't wait to fuck in a library. But in whispers to my Samantha (whom I still whispered to in eighth grade), I said the real reason. Maybe this could be the perfect experiment in controlled disappearing. Existing only when *I* wanted to. I knew that I felt like a living imaginary friend, a person who was only real when a passing protagonist needed a specific character. Then alone, invisible. Which was an embarrassing problem. Maybe a dorm room could be like an invisibility freezer drawer.

Also, the dark clouds of puberty loomed. I knew from Bunny and books that it was about to assign me an identity that so far sucked. Bunny was ready to at last live her Courtney Love truth at top volume in a new city-state. I was looking forward to boarding school being a Citibank lobby to wait out hail. I could privately finish suck-Hulking in the safety of an asylum with hedges. Oh and ice-cream-cake birthdays in the hallway. I remembered that from the tour and that seemed fun. When we got into different schools I breathed in hope.

My dad had gone to such a school in the sixties, and they still exist now, freckled across New England. Then they were mostly brick playpens for future senators, who said "gee" and hid sherry in the floorboards and swore oaths they'd never be senators. Now it's that still, with "fuck" instead of "gee," and Adderall-laced trust falls to raise awareness.

My mother was both proud and aghast. Having gone to school where nuns barked fear into her face and having lived poor in a house where a family member did the same, she could not believe life's turn that she was dropping her child at a school with a crest. Then I thought she was only tickled, which she was, but now I see there was something else. She dressed up for the day as a joke. Smuggling a joke into a milestone moment ensures you keep a foot in the river of *but not me, right?* (I flash to all the times on a red carpet I've thrown myself under the bus in an interview, performing self-loathing that was real but now treated like a party trick. *Oh really, Betty, you paid a publicist a mortgage and went through hours of hair and makeup because you* don't *like attention?*)

Today the joke was my mother dressed as a Stepford wife; a robin's-egg-blue sweater set and heirloom pearls and a velvet headband—askew for good measure. "Call me Mitsy!" Her usual garb was overalls and a faded T-shirt, spattered with garden or sawdust or contraband breakfast chocolate. But if a wink and an eye roll could hold hands in a little pageantry, she always seized it, and she played the part to drop her daughter off at Keats camp. I played *my* part of pretending to be embarrassed, but I loved it. Throughout my life her eccentricity was our *when the dog bites.* Her weird made things unscary. My mom.

Sadly my mother had misread this scene. Or unknowingly had got it just right. My new roommate was not a Daughter of Mitsy, but a scholarship student from the opposite of pastel-ed America. We walked in sporting our "making fun of boarding school" wear, the outfits of characters "*so* far from us" that we just happened to have the perfect costumes existing already in our wardrobe. Enveloping Jackie's mother in a hug, my mom scrambled to erase the sweater set cycling through distracting arm positions, all but saying, "Speaking of loofahs, you know, I had a *terrible* childhood."

Jackie and I taped up pictures in rows above our beds, quiet while her mother and my parents talked. Both her brothers were there, almost the exact age as my brothers, who were at home probably lighting Samantha on fire. They grabbed pictures out of Jackie's hands, disagreeing with the placement. I peeked over at the pictures—tiny Jackie in a backpack the size of a Jackie, posing with classmates in a fluorescent hallway, all pictures from the same day. Later, alone, staring at the pictures, I deduced it was a last day of school, in the days when you'd get a disposable camera and take the same picture over and over. (Other pictures went up after her mother left—Jackie with hair down, tube top the size of a wristwatch, sitting on various laps.) Her mother sobbed saying goodbye. Mine crossed her eyes and whispered our signature phrase that we now send to each other in opening-night cards:

"Don't embarrass me."

The first night was a crash course in shower choreography. It appeared that the girls with the novelty slippers and loudest boobs were permitted the first showers. Those of us who seared an I WANT TO DISAPPEAR hole in the hallway carpet during "Happy Birthday" to Ms. Carter's ancient beagle went last. I tiptoed to brush my teeth illegally past lights out, thinking I could thereby do it alone. I was wrong. A girl who I'd later learn was an Irish dancer and soprano wheeled in. Well, she *walked* in, but truly her feet had to be wheels because her walk was like a fucking *computer ghost* it was so even and mathematically floaty. It did not help that her skin was so white you could basically see her insides, like a human spring roll. It also didn't help that the oaky door screeched open like a vulture hovering over mass death. I screamed in her face, heaved a sob of guilt, shook her hand, and left the bathroom. Only when I'd sprinted back to my bed did I realize I'd never brushed my teeth.

After a few polite exchanges in the dark, Jackie and I said good night. The quiet ceiling. Then:

"Oh, you should know. My dad is out of jail. And he's looking for me."

Only now am I sure that across the room from my rattling frame, Jackie was shaking, too, laughing her ass off at the girl who thought she was so far from a Mitsy that her name was Betty.

I made friends in the way I know how to make friends—slip a subliminal eyebrow raise in an apology and see if they laugh. If they do, repeat. If they don't, *run*. I sat on the bed of one of the first ones who laughed, allowed for the first time in someone else's room. I had butterflies at the friend points. In an Aguilera impression I waved my "riff hand" too maniacally and spilled Fanta on her duvet cover. Orange liquid soaked a print fabric of, to my surprise, Muppet Babies. The vowel whine turned scream from the doorway told me it was not her duvet but that of her roommate, jetlagged from her fourteen-hour flight from Seoul. An anger-aria of Korean sang Mariah high and dropped earthquake low through her braces, a gorgeous language that I would hear lots of when we lived together years later in New York. But for now its beauty was lost on me. A particular sentence after a deep breath hung like a cloud, punctuated by a slow Marley's ghost point at my forehead. She slammed the door. In the resulting quiet my new friend breathed ". . . I think you just got cursed." I pretended to think she meant sworn at, but I knew she meant a spell.

Years later on our Houston Street fire escape, I asked Dani what she'd said all those years ago. She hit her perfectly rolled joint. She curled "oh, I don't remember" smoke into traffic as I watched the exact memory pass over her face in a smile. Later that day she peed while I showered, as boarding school forever dissolves certain boundaries while others are cemented. She pushed the curtain back from the toilet. "My *mother* made that blanket, and you disrespected it."

School was a huddle of buildings in a setting so pornographically green that later when we all returned from years of city life to get alcohol poisoning at the reunion, we screamed at the flora.

Collared shirts that covered your sinful parts and skirts down to the knee were ruler-eyed by looming deans, who knew before we did that we existed only to fuck each other and light property on fire. I was safe the first year, having packed for the dress code; I left my delinquent skater doll clothes at home. As a freshman I swam in boyish cargo pants and alternated two children's polos. It wasn't until later that I became sartorial enemy number one to Ms. Moncito, dressing like a Playmate in a mall fire to go to Chem.

This was not a girls-only school, thank God, or God help us. Half the dorms were filled with 100 percent Boy, gangly and pulsing and lost. A cluster of benches sat outside the freshmen boys' dorm, under a streetlamp like the one in Narnia. Unleashed from the dress code at night, the most daring of our Hall of Screechers put on their smallest elastic ho-shorts in the twilight after study hall and attempted a casual saunter across the grass. They posed through thigh splinters on those benches, sirening out interested parties in semen-caked track pants. By day we were puffy-eyed hand-raisers dressed for Easter Sunday. At night the thrill of wet hair and borrowed velour sweats that dipped below ovaries we didn't think about. We'd spill in a herd across the lawn toward the lamp at the benches, antelopes desperate to be speared. I sigh thinking at how much pageantry and forethought we put into this pilgrimage, spending the last half hour of study hall not reading but panicking over tank top hues under Liz G's *Party of Five* poster. I think of Steinbeck sitting crumpled and unread, watching me waste my education on wondering if Noah Fullerton liked a periwinkle boatneck or no.

Having two brothers I know that no such pageantry forethought existed in the boys' dorms. Boys showed up to class with hair like a cow cervix had just given it a once-over, in the same shirt day after day, toothbrushes lost at orientation and no search party assembled. Much of them spent the first semester dazed and tardy, a shock on their face when they found a classroom before a bell. But the girls were an army of questions and plotting, our dorms publicizing a process that for most girls existed alone behind a door. A recent farm documentary showed a lamb born with organs outside its little heaving body. *A girls' dorm,* I thought. Whatever experience that had been yours alone to flounder through was now dissected by a pajamaed committee, whether you liked it or not. Our second night we sat vigil around a stall while Lindsey Greenbaum brayed tampon insertion instructions to a sobbing other Lindsey. She screamed like it was a backward labor, Lindsey G her callous doula, herself apparently born with a Marb Light and teacher's manual.

When my FRIDAY printed underwear filled with blood the following Tuesday (I was never organized enough to get the days right), I tried to re-create Lindsey G's coaching on my own with a stolen tampon. I swallowed sobs through Am Civ but guessed it was supposed to feel like twenty Legos harpooning your nethers. Between classes I ran to my dorm to make sure my vagina had not been julienned. To my horror, the bathroom door swung into . . . *her.* The girl who was so beautiful that when she walked through the dining hall, silence fell around her like snow. For this reason I had avoided her like a poxy child. Turning her impossibly Marilyn body toward my sobbing lemur frame, she asked *what's wrong* like a detective made of angora. I described the pain of a tampon in an attempt to share a single Venn diagram overlap with this pinup archangel.

She put a teal-tipped hand on my shoulder.

"You left the plastic part in."

Hadley R's kindness bought my servitude. I spent freshman year carrying her books and shrinking from her rare curiosity. I shadowed her puberty like it was my first day of work in her section of a Cheesecake Factory. She shaved and did crunches, so I bought a Venus and a scale. The kings and queens of the jungle found each other and fumbled through virginity erasure; then we Timons and Pumbaas settled for our respective counterparts, mimicking milestones so as not to be eaten.

Or at least . . . I pretended to. I found a way to participate in group puberty with a half lie. I'd fill my quiver with boy-arrows like the rest of them, then nap in the hunter's blind, shrugging that bad luck and not fear accounted for my score of zero. But eventually a random jerseyed hormone would be threatened enough by my mumbled sarcasm that he'd invite himself over to my room or push me into a vestibule. I high-fived in the quad. In my room, I missed my mom.

Freshman year I auditioned for and didn't get a part in the fall Shakespeare, and instead entered the birth and death of my athletic career. "Thirds" soccer meant the team below junior varsity. It meant if your legs are strangers and your arms are enemies, then put on your cleats. My subs, meaning the two girls with interchangeable sports talent as me, were my duvet-stained enemy, Dani, and hallway ghost nightmare, Claire. The coach saw through me from the first practice, offering:

"You don't care about winning, do you, Gilpin?"

Ms. Holder cared very much about winning, and in retrospect I suggest she look inward at the non-win of forcing bookworms and goths to sprint until they puked.

After one such practice, Dani caught up with me on the sprawling meadow we took for granted.

"*Beech,*" she growled.

I looked up at her, bracing for another curse, when I saw she was pointing back at Holder alone on a bench. Dani blinked at me behind glasses that a starlet would select from a prop table to attempt a *wow-I-transformed* Oscar. Then she did the facial equivalent of my family crest. She crossed her eyes. I laughed in happy shock. A fellow fucking jester. I crossed mine. I took the other handle of the heavy cooler she'd been tasked with carrying as punishment for her innovative scrimmage tactic of sitting down on the ball. I taught her the word "horny." I held her when the captain of the lacrosse team microwaved her hamster. I called her last week to sing "Happy Birthday" in Korean to her second child.

Inconveniently, a high school dorm was not the invisibility closet I had hoped it would be. It was the opposite. I saw that feeling like a Rolodex of Selves for Others and having no clue who you were in a vacuum was not unique either. It was just being a girl. Outside in the maze of school and world we could perpetuate the Lie of Me—I was the book-carrying yesser, the apologizey joke-to-floor. But a bald and fluorescent society seized inside the dorm, where performance and armor were laughed away.

To my horror, a few girls crept into my life who saw the self I was hoping I could delete, and I saw theirs. Dani in braces and Carmen in dotted zit cream and Laura with the good chips. There were the people out there in the collared shirt sunlight who bought your ruse; then you'd go home to a handful of slippered sisters who had your number and asked you questions like, "Why do you let Hadley R talk over you?" "Why didn't you touch your soccer pizza?" And I asked illegal questions back. "Who's that in the picture?" "How old were you when . . . ?" "What if you waved *back* tomorrow? Shut up, you can." I saw how I had actively sought friendships where I could cower in the safety of their dominance. The dorm was the first place I learned friendship without visibility control. I couldn't choose when and how I existed to them; they saw the between-scenes moments that for thirteen years had been only mine. It was uncomfortable and horrible. The saddest part of female friendship is you see them exactly: unguarded and wonderful, gasping for air in the wings of the performance, and you want to shake them and say, "This, *this* is the best part of you," but then it's time for more performance and later you can't hear over your own gasps when they're screaming the same.

Things I was good at: peeing my pants for ten dollars at 3:00 a.m. in the stairwell to make my friends laugh, diverting the War of 1812 essay question to a relevant personal memory, seeking out corruption. Things I was bad at: nutrition, math, mirrors. By sophomore year the smallness I felt went from gee-whiz shyness to a self-hating darkness tilting the steering wheel over the centerline to see what would happen. Which . . . solved a lot of problems for me. I had spent so much time panicking that everyone *else's* lives had meaning and depth and mine had crickets and shrugs. Now came this thing that certainly felt like meaning. Maybe *this* was the identity I'd been searching for. Some people go to the Olympics, some crochet, I lie facedown on the tile next to my bed during lunch. Niche found!

Depression offered the option that my life was a disposable joke. That I didn't *need* to try for things because I didn't care about Alive. Blinking through the shinier ones' triumphs felt a little easier with a cyanide pill in my pocket. *Congrats on your blue ribbon.* I *don't need blue ribbons because I might go bye-bye tomorrow.* It was almost convenient. Other people were weighed down with self-love and goals—I didn't even need protein or safety! You get to treat the house like shit if you're only renting.

The perfect storm of *oh no* touched down when my depression's debutante ball coincided with the transfer of a nightmare from Jersey. A nightmare because you know the type: a backward hat leaning in a doorway shaking his head at you and wincing a forbidden soul orgasm "oof" sound like "you are an excruciating inconvenience to me." *That* guy. Before, the suitor choices had been coughing jocks who held their balls like Easter egg currency in Umbro shorts, feeling up the bony wiseass as a last resort, their flirting tactics ranging from insults to spanking. But *this* boy employed a tactic that the first time it's shined on you feels like smuggled wine at a Fox Newsy Christmas.

Instead of the familiar "you'll do if you stop with the puns," Anthony Moretti looked at me like I was a princess made for him. I made a *Dumb and Dumber* reference at a *Kiss Me Kate* rehearsal (the red-barned theatre department had finally let me in), and he looked up at me like I mentioned I lived in the little village where his massacred family was from. Any detail of my life that I gave him he smiled at like it was holy and winced like it hurt. Where his dorm mates had khakis and rage and yachty roots, he had ripped corduroys and agony and Jersey salt. He was re-cruited, I believe, for his talent—his misbehavior translating to stage presence and his singing voice making anklets out of your pants. He was a coveted new brand of boy that in college we'd all realize existed everywhere, like a hetero cancer, but he was our first, so our God for a while: a guitar-holding Pan whom you alone can fathom.

Daughter, *run*.

He held my face and kissed me under pianos for three years.

. . . No. That is revisionist shame. The actual time to trauma ratio is too mortifying to type. But . . . this is truth vomit so here we go.

He held my face and kissed me under pianos for three weeks. Three weeks. An amount of time apparently long enough to ruin someone's life.

He sang at *me* when his band played the Quad one weekend, his friends from home nauseous at our polos. He threw pebbles at my third-floor window to get my attention, like he was Romeo in suburbia. He fell to his knees dramatically when we passed each other on leafy walkways. But by the time sweaters were unpacked, I watched his breath come out in frozen clouds as he explained he had to be free. Apparently free to fuck Melanie Pilaticini the next day, and free to methodically hold the faces of every mascara owner on campus, sighing that their adorability was his curse and telling them they were royalty under pianos.

My junior-year dorm room faced the building with the pianos. I left my window open on purpose, bathing in misery, my bedroom echoing with his singing Ben Folds to whatever scrunchied fellater was his that week. It was *torture*.

The dormant inherited darkness in me had sat patient for its entrance excuse, and Anthony Moretti breaking my heart was its *You're on, Plath*. I plummeted into a sea of wanting to be dead, a sea that took me a long time to realize was not a reaction but a preexisting condition. Women's darkness is so much more inevitable and interesting than a broken heart; it's just sometimes the thing that gets us there. Figuring out how to use it as a super-power is the tricky part.

Theatre came close. In the first year I'd been sleeve pulling and red-cheeked, prepubescent in every category. But now heartache made me a thousand years old and a ghost alive. Channeling it into Shakespeare for two hours a day was the only upside. I held a skull borrowed from Bio and sobbed into its sockets, my voice-cracking castmates disturbed at the authenticity of my screams to the rafters. I realized that acting wasn't just about chasing the feeling of singing *South Pacific* into my mother's cookie-dough beater. It was also the perfect illegal marriage of Salem and Barbie—using the churning dark in your performed self. Fleeting moments of an open trapdoor in public. So much of being sixteen was screaming "See *this* part not *that*" to blindfolded people. Looking back, I realize theatre saved my life. I don't mean that in a hyperbolic, scarfed woman talking about her manicurist way. I mean if I were a runt chipmunk speed-walking on MDMA in the dust bowl, the theatre department was a little rodent-electrolyte gas station.

Theatre was a few tiny seconds of being seen for exactly who I was.

Sophomore year I got into bed, and my foot hit a cold thing. I threw back the comforter and found vodka and a note.

Come downstairs.

Two seniors who deemed me funny and pitiful waited for me on the second floor and ushered me into a room of bloodshot

French braids. The funnest, baddest mother's nightmares there were. I had friends upstairs who wanted to know me unhidden—but that self was becoming a not fun person to be. Normally I would hide in servitude; here I could hide in inebriation. I made the thrilling original discovery that being stoned and drunk was better than being bored and sad. I started spending all my time with these bunned outlaws. We huddled in closets blowing smoke into water bottles filled with dryer sheets, then made our noses blue with Adderall remembering that the SATs were in six hours and we had to focus. In one six-hundred-year afternoon's mushroom trip, we stumbled out of the woods into a Revolutionary War reenactment. A fucking real one. Six of us stood frozen in a line, tits shaking in halters at every cannon blast, a redcoat's Reeboks my only solace that we hadn't teleported.

Dani and Carmen and Laura slept soundly while I crept down to the *yikes.* My new friends bobbed in the first-floor hallway waiting for whoever couldn't sleep or cope. We cut through a window screen and snuck to the boys' dorm at 3:00 a.m., sprinting through the snow in a line so teachers couldn't count footprints come sunup. Probably Mr. Pearson watched, eye-rolling from his apartment, the ten of us shivering in clubwear, risking our futures to blow Camel smoke in the boys' shower vent.

Anthony Moretti was in the moonlit cluster of pajamaed boners waiting for us with the door propped. As I passed him, I looked up at his smirk, his eyebrow raised that I was there with the big kids, wearing risk like a costume where it was part of his skin. We all leapt up the stairs in disbelief at our collective gall, grabbing at each others' asses in the dark. Ten of us huddled whispering in the bathroom. I leaned against a boy I didn't like to telegraph indifference. When Anthony disappeared to his room with a girl I had a shared bracelet with, the leaned-on boy put a hand on my shoulder. I reluctantly turned to reciprocate the advance but realized in a bald fluorescent moment he was just . . . comforting me. I took a bong hit that would have killed a colt and blew it out the window into the flurries.

The rest of high school was this. We lay on our backs seeing cartoons in the rafters. In an attempt to appear unpathetic to the giggling student body, I romantically pursued a few human shrugs that weren't Anthony. I would banter with various neighboring Patagonia-ed cavemen on AOL and avoid them in real life, but for the rare trysts where we crossed party lines and jock fondled stoner. But rare it was; I was not their cup of tea. If a coughing lacrosse-person was bored and curious and none of the Julias were IMing him back, he would waddle over to my room where suddenly in person I had nothing smart-ass to say. We were aliens to each other. I must have been profoundly unfun.

You were allowed to sign a boy into your room from 9:15 to 10:00 p.m., between study hall and lights-out. The only rule was you had to prop the door open and have three feet on the floor. So that, naturally, a girl could cross her legs. We all graduated with our first sexual experiences occurring as fast as possible behind elaborate tapestried bunk bed cabanas, a hairy seventeen-year-old foot in an Adidas sandal slamming onto the linoleum if you heard an approaching clipboard. This blow job may be terrible, but by God, we have three feet on the floor, don't we?

After a few "not much haha" AOL exchanges, Jeremy Asher told me to come to his room, so I did. There he played chopsticks on my visible ribs and asked why I wore the same pants every day. I blinked a Morse code response. Because my tenth-grade visible ribs fit Hadley R's sixth-grade giveaway pile, because I suddenly put nutrition in the vanity category, because five oyster crackers apparently hit the spot, and I'm sorry my hair smells like a hundred cigarettes, I bet the Julias' hair smells like honeysuckle cookies. He received the blink of Help I'm Sad as a Fuck You I'm Bored, a messaging error my blinks send to this day. He raspberried my growling stomach. I wished my belly button was pierced. We made out.

He pulled back from the kiss, and terror fell across his face like I'd splashed it from a wineglass.

"I'll be right back."

To make sure it wasn't my baseline hideousness that had sent him running to the bathroom, I looked in the mirror. My face was covered in blood—his blood. The narcissism of self-hate turned it immediately into *my* problem, not his, and with a found T-shirt and water bottle I scrubbed terrified at my face before he could return. When he came back, I was posing casually on his bed, both our faces church clean and hearts pounding in fear that the other would ask the Kryptonite illegal question: "Are you OK?" You could never be too careful—you never knew when something as simple as a nosebleed could out us as children.

I didn't understand how I could feel both mortifyingly naive and snarkily jaded in all the wrong ways. Living at your high school meant there was no space to go home alone and reset, no time to catch your breath alone with your dolls and remember you were a person before all this and would be after. No parent noticing you put four cucumber slices and a tablespoon of Raisin Bran on your plate for every meal. No meeting the eyes of a worried sibling in the hallway when you chugged an entire bottle of cough syrup—just the saucery dilation of a fellow hallucinating insomniac nodding maniacally when you suggest trying to crawl on the roof.

The girls I'd deemed sisters were confused. At thirteen we snuck into each other's rooms and admitted we were homesick and lip-synced to Spice Girls and wrote in Sharpie on the closet ceiling that we'd never separate. Now we were seventeen, and they liked volleyball and dance and homework, and I liked drugs and saltines. They loved me but didn't know how to help. I still crawled to their rooms for snuggly DVDs but now was permahigh and frail. Theatre could have been my *see-me* vessel, but Anthony was in all the plays, too, and my public decent into Salem-y heartbreak overshadowed my monologue choices. The senior boys made Jerry Springer reaction noises when Anthony Moretti and I had to kiss in *As You Like It,* everyone aware of the mortifying history of my swearing allegiance to a king who didn't want me.

I still feel mortification like ice in my spine when I think of Anthony Moretti as Romeo and me as . . . Paris, crumpled dead in a purple turban next to Anthony and Kayla Sherman passionately dry humping in the final scene. At the cast party they re-created this tableau with sleeping bags and reality. On the walk to World History the next morning, Dani asked the still-great question: "Why didn't Mr. G let you die stumble? Walk offstage?" But Dani knew, too, with her rubber band braces and misplaced plurals, you don't get to choose when you're in the wings.

I got one year of Anthony-less theatre when he graduated. It wasn't much different. In the cafeteria I was a human lockbox; then onstage I was an open chasm. I was playing guarded and not hungry out there and then literal Hamlet onstage, memorizing soliloquies in the rare sober hours. The nerdy Laertes knew his lines day one and blinked at my shoes when I cried in rehearsal. My public persona had gone from Trusty Ham to Sarcastic Ice. I felt like neither, and wondered if anyone could tell me what I actually was. I was mortifyingly desperate to be described.

My costume sagged off me. The school counselor left a voice-mail on my parents' machine that she'd had several reports that I was not eating, a surprise to me that this, too, was a public story line in the group gawk. It felt like wearing a wool cape and no pants—the rare parts of me I liked invisible, and the ugliness so visible it was apparently for sale.

Only now do I see the education itself was the rarest gift that I shat all over, showing up stoned to 70 percent of it. Small groups debating Freud and Austen around oak tables, our feet sparring flirtation below while our fingers drummed innocence above. Instead my focus was on drowning out my embarrassment that my failures and demons seemed to play out like an interactive tele-novela for the whole school. And worst of all, I hid from friendships I didn't recognize. I snuck downstairs away from the girls who wanted to ask questions. I ran through snow toward people I could fool.

The last week of senior year I got a folded note. It was a riddle. My dad on the phone unlocked the verbal code that without his help in this Google-less world would have stopped the game there. But a decimal was apparently a batting average of a player with an obscure name, the name of our Science Center, and as promised, under the lab's lone cactus, the second clue waited for me.

My heart pounded with who it could be. At last in this final

week I was being promoted to romantic redemption arc instead
of pie-faced pity. Every clue was complicated and brilliant and
often took a committee of my girlfriends screaming over theories
in bunk beds to untangle. The A students and the hallucinators had
two things in common: we were all bored and horny. So much
so that we were covered in hickeys from each other, not from
romance, but from boredom. We ambushed each other in hallways like Nerf gun fights, but with our mouths. It was so fucking
dumb. So senior spring we were a horrifying leper colony of hormones, arms and faces Dalmatianed in sexual boredom. "WHAT
IF IT'S ANTHONY?" screamed a Lindsey from the doorway, a
hickey impossibly on her *eyelid*. My stomach turned both at the
luck that I hadn't sucked Lindsey's actual eyeball into my trachea
when I scarred her so and that I knew that as much as I wanted
it to be, this wasn't him. The final clue instructed me to leave a
penny in the windowsill of the dining hall if I wanted the truth.
We sprinted to breakfast and left five dollars in pennies against
the glass, all of us emptying our drawers anyway, our parents en
route to collect the children they'd dropped off four years ago.

Alone I went to the final reveal, to the empty school chapel
as instructed. I stopped in an inhale, squinting confused at who
stared back at me. Not a rose-holding linebacker, but a seven-
inch Mr. Potato Head doll, formal and plastic. It stood on a letter.

I read the letter with a certain talent we all have, that when
something is too painful or true we can just erase it in real time.
And I did. The words just kind of thudded against my brain
like gulls on a Tribeca high rise. I sighed at the autograph. It was
the blinking boy who had played Laertes to my Hamlet, a strange
lisping genius whom I didn't know at all. I had a vague idea that
he was a sober day student and had a 4.0, and those two facts of

course meant we hadn't exchanged more than six words in four years, apart from iambic pentameter. I found him in the cafeteria and hugged him *goodbye* and *thanks* and left school.

A decade after its delivery, I found the Mr. Potato Head letter. It was crumpled in the back of my bedside table drawer, with an empty cigarette pack and friendship bracelets of people who were pregnant now. Rereading the letter, I felt sick. I remembered it as a buzzing inconvenience, a weirdo I didn't know proclaiming his crush on the last day of school. That my narcissism and repression collaborated on this interpretation deserves a Lie Pulitzer. Maybe high school for everyone is clinging to people who can't see you and waving away those that insist they do. Trying on, *is this me? This? Or this?* And seeing only years later that it was the between yous that stuck; there *were* people who saw the self you assumed was vapor. That as much as you tried to control it, you existed out loud the whole time. At least to someone.

I sat down on the floor of my childhood bedroom and read the letter. A face-down Samantha frozen in abandoned time where I left her at thirteen listened to me sob at how wrong I'd gotten it.

It wasn't a love letter. It was just a description. You are this. You are this, too. This is nice. This is funny. This is important. This isn't. This is visible to me. You are visible to me. I'm glad we met.

7

THE THING

Throughout my childhood my father put us through a sort of screamy bird-watching school of film, standing in the center of the living room shouting, "Now WATCH" as if before we had been pointing our scalps at the screen, unsure why we couldn't see Brando. My hippocampus has permanently braided his commentary into the films themselves, and I'm not sure I know the difference. I fear the day when I watch *On the Waterfront* after he's gone, and no one is screaming into my ear, "Now LOOK—*LOOK!*" when Eva Marie Saint drops her glove, a 1954 blooper that made the cut.

"*Watch,*" Dad barks. "She's flustered, 'Uh-oh, should we start again?' And Brando just *picks it up*—" and now Dad's tone shifts from admiral on an on-fire horse to gentle prince at the funeral of a sparrow, whispering a eulogy into a birdhouse: ". . . he takes her glove . . . and he puts it on."

And sure enough, unscripted, Brando stops. He changes the blocking, stooping for her glove and plopping down on a swing. He then wriggles his concussion-doling hand into her little elf-sized glove. It transforms the air in the scene, so much so that watching it I feel like a prop assistant there on the day, stomach churning from fear and then an eerie awareness that suddenly we're in Oz. There's freedom and risk and sexiness all over it, in an era of film that could be so stiff and chaste.

I recently rewatched the scene for the first time as an adult. I couldn't believe what I was seeing. It is a perfect example of something so inexplicable and fleeting—a thing that is very, very rare to capture. People lose themselves trying to.

Beneath the physical language of the scene, they start to do The Thing. A strange sort of portal is accessed between them, enabling little buried internal parts of them to, impossibly, communicate. In the real world, these internal parts, or internal people, are invisible. Muffled. But here in the scene, some magic code has been accessed. A clear channel between their souls opens up. And the once invisible parts . . . wave at each other. And talk.

Watching it happen in this particular scene is fascinating. In a way that only Brando could, he wrenches closed his internal door to roiling machismo and power, and instead suddenly lets a little curious boy against that door do the talking. Brando treats Saint's character's life details as the most important things in the scene, little holy clues, like stumbly fawns he can coax out from the thicket if he's gentle enough. She slowly realizes she's speaking to the boy and not the brute. Against her better judgment, she allows him a little window into her person in an otherwise shades-drawn life. He recalls her former braces and braids, asks about her dreams, an unspoken telegram of *I've seen you this whole time.* Then he dances away from that vulnerability, offering an aside that nuns tried to abuse an education into him "but I foxed 'em." (How Brando could make PTSD light and sexy is an essay unto itself.) But Saint knows the suspendered boy hasn't disappeared back behind the lout yet. She slides a tiny note to him under the machismo door that *she* would have taught him with "patience, and kindness. That's what makes people mean and difficult. People don't care enough about them."

And then escapes her first and only smile of the scene, a prize so dissolving that Brando has to physically walk away.

That's The Thing.

It's a rare connection impossible to explain, and perhaps sort of illegal to name. But I'm going to try, because it's my favorite thing in a world where souls are kept shrouded in personas and aesthetics. Well, it's my favorite thing when used correctly. In the right hands it's a portal to meaning. One wrong turn and it's a threat to your life.

The reasons for becoming an actor are varied and mostly embarrassing. They include but are not limited to:

1. tap-dancing to right the wrongs of your childhood
2. putting on hats to stave off meaninglessness
3. channeling your trauma and weird into memorization for cab fare

   But also the one that matters most:
4. Trying to achieve, even once a decade, The Thing.

I remember reading a Scientology defector's memoir about the moment you have earned your way into secret knowledge, allowed after years of hoops and dollars to open some obscure locked briefcase filled with the coveted truth. The first time you feel this Thing I'm talking about as an actor, it feels like this moment. Except it's not a huge letdown that you've given your children's tuition money to Avon for Aliens, but . . . something so magnificent and dangerous that you are sure you are the only person who's ever felt it and if you named it you'd explode.

It is the feeling of standing across from someone and having all the opposite brainpeople—except a single impossibly *identical* one. These brain-twins stare out your eyes through a conversation at each other, hand illegally outstretched in wonder. Time stops. Neuroses and circumstance fall away. It's just a clear channel of communication from your deepest self to theirs. Impossibly and suddenly, you are *deeply known by a relative stranger*. Because you are saying someone else's words and wearing someone else's clothes, the normal hurdles of intimacy are disabled, and what would take years for a friend to know is given to a stranger for free.

For some reason your soul takes the presence of a prop table as license to spread its butt-cheeks for catharsis.

I mean, listen. Most of the time acting is just two narcissists doing Voices and Faces, and no science-defying secret communion occurs. But every once in a while you glimpse it: the heroin of inexplicable connection with someone. It feels like magic.

Your job as an actor is to bypass normal getting-to-know-you checkpoints in the name of pretend. You're not sure where your scene partner is from, but you somehow know what happened when they were six, or that if pushed, they'd be capable of murder, and what their eyes look like in both instances. Two grown-ups simulating humanity in the name of fiction is mortifying and difficult. Making the fake feel real is hard. Acting can feel like trying to coax a ghost into a room, a ghost that will flee if there are coughs or candy-wrapper sounds or your own thoughts or the wrong socks that day. Different actors have different ways of attempting to conjure this ghost. Some have enough IMDb credits to insist the entire crew call them by their character's name. Some scream that the way the air-conditioning is blowing is surely to blame for the first take sucking. Some listen to music or flirt with the sound guy to keep it loose.

(Me? Oh. Um. Sometimes backstage or in my trailer I uh . . . I look at pictures of the dead bodies at Jonestown on my phone. You know, to tell the ghost she can come in. Considering cancelling therapy because I'm fixed!)

There's also a lot of feeling invisible in the long stretches between these fleeting moments of Yes. You try to conjure the ghost with a gum-chomping casting intern while their boss peruses the lunch menu and yawns through the choice you thought would hush the room. A review of what you thought was your opus skips over your presence in the piece entirely or waves you off as "the endearing" or "a shrill" misspelled version of your name, and you die a little, realizing that being seen by someone who doesn't understand you feels even more invisible than never being looked at at all.

So then these tiny Moments, the looking up and seeing someone seeing you, the specific part of you that you've been trying to shake the world by the collar and make them recognize, the part that maybe your family doesn't get and that first boyfriend wanted to eradicate, the part that you thought was yours alone— seeing someone wave to it like it's the best most obvious part of you is an unexpected ecstasy pill in line at the dentist. It's God.

From what I understand, at normal jobs, there are labeled soups and headphones and boundaries. You notice Ken has a rash because there's no team of makeup illusionists to hide Ken's rash.

You notice Grace is covered in iguana dandruff and has a framed picture of Ted Bundy, and when she espouses her troubling theory about the postal service, you know not to say yes to lunch. There is normal time and space for red flags to emerge. You didn't confide your trauma to Don in marketing because that would be inappropriate, and you'll never know that Don cries in his car over someone he can't forget because why would Don tell you that.

But if they were actors, you'd know all of it on day three. In the ruse of achieving The Thing, actors mow down boundaries, desperate to connect, addicted to the notion that these people don't know about your eczema and bad credit but see you as the music video version of yourself that you can convince them you really are. Together you can access a little island away from the world. Safe here in the bubble of make-believe, you are each other's ticket to The Thing.

I have had many connections like this in my career. I have had the privilege of seeing a stranger for exactly who they are and holding that secret like a prized shell you keep in your drawer to remember how it felt to find it.

But if you do find it—beware.

This gift can be abused. Using the shelter of a creative environment to bypass boundaries to find a shared brainperson with arms outstretched and defenses disabled is a skill. Those capable can use it both as church and as a drug. You can, too. I have. Soul-connection wise, it's easy to confuse communion with crack. Realizing you're on either side of the betrayal is painful.

There are different types of The Thing. To both protect you from and push you toward the danger, let's walk through them.

TYPE 1: When You Think They Think You're a
Haunted Genius but Actually

With men, or whomever you fancy, it's triply complicated, because of course by the laws of Zeus and Newton, everyone wants to fuck each other.

Because so much of The Thing is unspoken, it is easy to realize too late that you are not in agreement on what that specific connection means. There have been times when I thought we were both participating in a mutual communion of *fuck the world, all that exists is the work,* and for that reason only we must poetically dissolve personal boundaries. A holy platonic *we are the same.* These were times where I thought we were magnificently on the same page. Then I come to work ready to continue the ceremony of unspoken soul intertwining on behalf of art and suddenly get a text from across the room from the man who I thought was my fellow monk in metamorphosis of spirit, but instead of speaking in the ancient language I thought we discovered together he says "Cool, so when's my blow job."

These are times where you realize what was magic for you was just them humoring you until you finally pulled down your jeggings. That the character they brain-cast you as wasn't Virginia Woolf as a sorceress, it was chorus girl number sixty-two. Sixty-two because instead of this being unlike any moment in time for them, this was like sixty-one other moments and would be like seventy thousand others.

This one is its own strange heartbreak. You thought you'd achieved the elusive platonic mirroring of spirit, only to realize too late you're sorely mistaken.

Strangely I've had this most with older men. Even, bluntly . . .

old men. Men so grandpappy-esque that I stupidly thought sex was about as on the table as cannibalism. I doubt any of them would read a book I wrote, most of them too ego-soaked to read anyone else's memoir but their own, but if they are reading this they are shifting uncomfortably, ready to call their lawyer. Hun? Relax. There were seven to twelve of you and I'm going to be vague. Just as I was one of many to you.

There are even specific details that apply to all of you; the Venn diagram overlap is wide and pathetic. Sighing with eyes wince-closed and shaking your head when I made a pun, pretending every woman you'd met before me was illiterate and you'd been making puns alone in a vacuum for decades until this moment. I make a Zero Mostel joke, and your face contorts in condescending amazement like I had gotten up from a wheelchair to tap-dance. Stained cardigans that I filed under Evidence of Genius, then post–fondling attempt I realize were Evidence of Sad Dad. Texts that I thought were the furious exchange of ideas and meaning and escape from the mundane I realize now were probably one of five threads you had going to see which would get you to fellatio first.

Thankfully I never took any of these grumbly auteurs up on their suggestion that we pivot from intellectual collaboration to Motel Fumblings. (I swear. I didn't.) But it embarrassingly always came as a shock. I'd cry on the subway picking apart the transcripts of our synthesis that I thought redefined friendship and mind melding, and instead was suddenly so baldly ordinary. As if Obi-Wan turned to Luke and said, "OK, great, for your last lesson put down the saber, lift up the kimono, let's finally see dat ass."

Every time I wondered where I had gone wrong. By this point

I had already gone through the plot-twist second puberty where at eighteen my body morphed from Oliver Twist to Pamela Foghorn. I wrote it off that the Marilyn aspects of my body sent these men signals I didn't intend to send—that big tits turning toward you to contest your point about Chekhov can be a misleading signal, seeming to be a blinking sign that I'm Trying to Fuck when actually it's just a part of my body that's also there and insists on always being there, like a shadow or stage mom. Or did I send my response pun text too far after dinnertime? I'm nineteen and don't understand clocks. I guess when you're fifty-seven and you get a funny text at 1:00 a.m., it's different from a logistical text at noon. But our correspondence and work together felt so much more important and soaring than flirtation.

Most embarrassing of all, I thought they thought I was brilliant. Just as brilliant as them. And, drunk with this lie, my ego deleted all incoming warning signs that they didn't think I was a genius; they thought I was proof of theirs. Not Patti to their Mapplethorpe, but Stormy to their Donald.

. . . Ugh, or. Or was my self-worth so low that I knew exactly what was happening? That I didn't know how to seek out respect for my brain without the guaranteed drug of being adored? One is risk; the other is a safety net. Maybe I was afraid that my soul alone was too measly of a prize and presented on its own would expose it as unexceptional. It had to be paired with the surefire hit of being *wanted*. Maybe I knowingly painted myself as whatever Lost Pixie Duck they thought me to be. Letting them own the details of my life as color for their memoir chapter felt like I was writing my own, but I wasn't. I was just keeping myself as a titted cameo in theirs, on hold in the ether for the rest of the book, making writing my own impossible. I certainly didn't think they would actually *pursue* me. I just assumed they could quietly think I was glittery, that our connection and the work still towered above something as cheap as their suggesting they cheat on their wives. They did not feel this way. I'm sure they still don't.

OK, fun, next type!

TYPE 2: Ready to Set My Life on Fire Because I've Found Religion in a Fuckable Stranger

Hoo boy. If you find yourself in the midst of this one . . . my prayers are with you. The horrors of full-on mutual infatuation in the workplace. This is the kind where your vagina thinks she's invited to the séance and has a meltdown when you try to tell her she isn't. Disabling this genitalic tantrum before it's too late is a skill every actor has to learn to hone, and they're lying if they tell you it's never been a problem. (*You,* there, hi, you are a liar.) Since it will happen seventeen thousand times in your career, you just have to become an expert in identifying signs that you're in the *we are art soul twins and also I want to fuck you should we maybe fuck for the art* danger zone and tuck and roll out of that Rocketship to Pain the second you realize you're on board.

Of course, by all means sleep with whomever you want. My good God: do it, babe. Just know in a *work* setting, Type 2 has the potential to muddy the pure form of The Thing. The beautiful kind. The one that makes your work better and soul richer. Clouding it with infatuation does not enrich art: it repels it. No matter what you and what's-his-scarf are telling yourselves. Holding hands and meaningfully breathing heavy backstage does not make the scene better. It makes it worse.

There is only so much time in the workday. When there is a coworker distracting your nethers, there is less brainpower and time to achieve creative nirvana. That time is now spent crafting an illusion separate from the illusion you're being paid to craft. A double life inside a double life. It's harder to be a good Hamlet when you're focused on being Fantasy You on every ten-minute break instead of looking over your graveyard scene.

On an acting job, you get to live in a montage world where you're tailored and painted into a fantasy version of yourself. Watching a hot coworker buy the lie that that's *actually* you is intoxicating. You're not a manual of creaks and mistakes; you're a poem that's only ever existed now. And you buy *their* lie, too—the little revealed slivers of who they "really are" between scripted and costumed moments. It becomes your drug. Every little anecdote or overheard song in their headphones or boots with a backstory is a clue in an addictive mystery. You curate your own clues in turn. In between scripted moments of playing a character you are . . . playing a character. For him.

Because you're going to Greek and apocalyptic stakes in scenes together, and cracking open your ribs to bear your soul with no normal protective checkpoints, you tell yourself you really *know* this person. You begin to fill in vague blanks of their life with your imagination and write a story about who they are. But it's not *them* you're falling in love with—it's you. You're addicted to the *you they think you are*. A you so much more exciting than the you, say, unemployed and bloated, with bad posture.

That you is not great. It's uncomfortable. And *this*? Is so fucking *easy*. In a scene, or giggling at a crafty table, and knowing the job is only for a bubble of time, you don't have to earn loving each other by learning each other because all the boring legwork is being done for you. It's a Disney FastPass past red flags and boundaries that coworkers in a cubicle would spot from a mile away. You wave off his temper because you *know* the hurt seven-year-old at the root of it. So what if he turned over a table when the lighting took too long—*you alone know what happened to him at camp.* The not showering is easy to forgive when you don't share a lease and don't have to dwell that it's probably an indicator that he doesn't pay taxes or go to the dentist. Because you share a brainperson with him, because there's a laser of light that pulses between you when a scene is going well or when your eye contact and nod backstage or before *action* felt like Meaning so much more vital and gorgeous than your life before. Red flags can be waved away in the name of poetry.

If you are bored and overlooked in your logistical grocery store life, a connection like this feels like a vaccine against *blegh.* You get to chop away the seaweed tangles tying your ankles to the bottom of the sea and swim freely for a few hours a day. In your apartment, you are a shackled manatee trying to avoid sugar and screening calls from your mother. But now, here, at *work,* you are a vibrating mermaid backflipping through space and capacity for feeling. (Listen, if you haven't picked up that the metaphors are going to be mixed and the commas are going to be pandemical, I don't know what to tell you. I suggest *The Sun Also Rises,* which has no commas or vulnerability but a great list of what time they ate.)

Before we move on to Type 3, just a general programming note. I *know* it feels like you invented it or that This Time It's Different.

With the utmost Steinem respect and Scary Spice #girlpower, I say to you, my sister: It's. Just. Not.

When the job is over, when the spell is broken, and you hear all the horror stories that sound a lot like yours, clarity and perspective will be a cold pail of water in your face. But like childbirth, your brain will erase the memory and you'll do it again.

This is why—gather close, girls, come sit at my buckled shoe, put down your tea, and crumple your hoop skirt near your old mother so I may whisper to you the simple truth that hath been writ on the inside of sparrows' wings for centuries—DO NOT FUCK HIM, YOU FUCKING IDIOT. DO. NOT. FUCK. HIM. DONOTFUCKHIM. YOU THINK IT'S SPECIAL BUT IT'S NOT. IT IS NOT SID AND NANCY, IT'S NOT RICHARD BURTON AND ELIZABETH TAYLOR, IT'S AN AGING KEVIN MCCALLISTER IN GOODWILL LEATHER AND YOU ARE SHIRLEY TEMPLE IN BAD COURTNEY LOVE DRAG, HE IS NOT A MISUNDERSTOOD PORN POET AND NEITHER ARE YOU, HE'S A DOUCHE IN A HAT AND YOU'RE A TART IN A WIG CAP, GO. HOME. AND. MASTURBATE. UNTIL. THE FEELING. DIES.

Which it will. I promise. Mortifyingly fast.

. . . Or, you know, *go for it.* Is life too short to light fires or to *not* light them? I'm tired.

TYPE 3: Impossibly, Her

Every actor has another actor whose name makes them want to throw dishes. Who when your agent tells you *she* got the job, your mouth says, *That's fine,* but your left eye shrinks to a raisin while the right bulges to a melon, and huh, your nails have engraved NO in a nearby wall. No matter what "level" you are at, you are always the little bit worse version of someone else. And if you forgot, the business lets you know, over and over and over again.

When you are an actress, your brain can really run with the idea that your nemesis is a monster. Most scripts read like this: seven men exchange paragraphs, *one* girl enters in pleather and says seven *words.* The opportunity to *work* with your she-peers instead of evil-eyeing each other across a waiting room is rare. I had, like everyone, my list. When I first started out there was a particular blue-eyed savant who just could not stop robbing me of my destiny. This was back before I learned you were supposed to hang up before your agent hears you cry. But then I sobbed into my Nokia, "It was supposed to be *me!!!*" Another one had brown eyes and *way* better comic timing. *And* could play piano, *and* sing, *and* emote, *and* mix patterns without it looking like a circus fire. There was another who was ice in waiting rooms and obviously that meant she deserved ice back. Often you are delivered the word-for-word blunt societal reality of why you didn't get a part. Why you're not their person. Your face, your weight, your age, your *way.* Instead of directing your fury at the system that makes you feel speck-like, you instead direct it at . . . *her.*

Every time I work with a *her,* every single fucking time, I hate it. I hate it because I fall in love. After years of cursing her name, I did a play with the brown-eyed one. We showed up to rehearsal on the first day wearing the same thing—a navy zip-up hoodie, ripped jeans, and Converse. I rolled my eyes. Great, we're the same. Just as this business drills into us over and over again. But as we slowly let ourselves know each other, I saw I was wrong. We certainly had the brain-twin of course, making each other choke-laugh voicing sidewalk dogs between two-show-days. But the revelation of this particular type is not the sameness but the vast intricate oppositeness. On casting emails and bulletin boards you are listed as indistinguishable, Doll 1 and Doll 2. Now you learn that while you always knew *you* weren't a doll but an *ocean,* you see she is an ocean, too, with entirely new depths and tides that you never paused your sulking to consider. The brown-eyed one was complicated and hilarious and masterful in ways I couldn't touch. And I had almost missed it. The icy waiting room girl and I played glorified extras in a movie about child murder, having to sob together out of focus in the background of the lead bro's monologue. I walked in wondering what we would talk about. By hour two I was ready to google how to change my surname to hers. Later there was a glittery movie star whose body and face made you never want to see a bikini or mirror again, and I'd flip off her name when it was on posters of movies I'd wanted. After years of poster-spiting, we did one job together. Now we talk every day, because of course hovering above her beautiful body is her beautiful fucking brain, writhing with ideas that make me like the world more.

I did a play that the evil blue-eyed one wrote—my original enemy number one. (So much so that my boyfriend in seeing her name on page 1 and knowing my hatred said, "Oh God, are you *sure?*") But I read her words and put my head in my hands. I realized she was scared of and longed for all the same things I did, but she voiced them in a way I never could. She was not a vile tart. She was brilliant. After one rehearsal we walked downtown from the theatre on Fifty-fourth Street and just kept not getting on the subway, that particular New York New Friend walk that pairs have probably been doing for eons. This was a woman who I had literally prayed would find a new hobby and new planet. Now my stomach flipped when we walked by the West Fourth Street train entrance, desperate to learn more about this multilayered woman I'd written off as a one-dimensional girl. When I caught her hopeful smile when we walked past Chambers Street, it was better than a crush. It's the same smile my goddaughter would give me years later when offered ice cream, fizzy hope elbowing past hesitancy, identical to her mom.

Now when I lose a role to one of the *hers,* I shake my fists at the email and not the woman. *How, how can you think we are the same?*

OK. On to the hardest one.

TYPE 4: Something Harder to Explain

I did a play that wasn't very good, which isn't betraying anything specific because I have done about four billion of those. This one went on for months in a mostly empty theatre in Midtown, a thousand "when will this be over" coughs punctuating every matinee. But I was fresh out of college and thought the coughs were marvelous. There was a hole in the dressing room wall, an aggro-renovation from the fist of an enraged movie star, upset from a *Long Day's Journey* note session. I touched it daily for luck with reverence.

I shared this dressing room with an older lady named Carol.

Outside our weird puppet jobs Carol and I would never have found each other. Honestly, we would never be friends. Carol was forty years older than me and lived an opposite life. I was still in my unfortunate chapter where I was perpetually stoned with a mostly Lycra wardrobe, posing with tangled headphones on subways to try to make hungover bassists and roidy bankers fall in love with me and then run yelping if they crossed the platform to actually talk. I was twenty-three and chasing the feeling of being adored with no accountability. I was sarcastic and selfish.

Carol lived on the same train line as me, alone with her two corgis, and Carol had had a *life*. She had stumbled and weaved, singing loud on the same blocks I now stumbled and weaved on, but had learned her lesson long ago, righting the ship and walking steady long before I met her. Her life was quiet and careful and smart. Mine was loud and frantic and unwise.

The first day, I could feel our differences pulsing. Day one of a play rehearsal is somewhat of a social nightmare anyway. It's before the actual acting part and is instead just scarfed creatives awkwardly shuffling with bagels, nodding at costume sketches and mortifyingly attempting what we are all terrible at—normal small talk. I shudder to think of my cleavaged and jegginged self glazing over at Carol's questions, a sixtysomething-year-old woman offering me no hint of validation so why would I commit her birthday or address to memory? I'm hoping she had her version of the same, a deserved eye roll at a cheekboney brat who seemed to think wearing two different color Converse outsourced a personality.

Then we acted together.

The play itself was a little silly and a little trite, as near-dead patrons would tell us aloud from the creaking dark. But it had some beautiful moments. The first time I looked up at Carol in our train scene, I felt a weird ice laser go through my eye, sent beaming from hers. Together in the outside world, we stammered and didn't make sense. But here in pretend we were made for each other. The pretext of a play allowed us to slough off our carefully curated opposing identities. We instantly understood that buried inside . . . we were the same. The *exact* same. A jaunty little gagged and bound elf waving at his twin from their respective dungeons on our spleens, allowed suddenly to revel together, unsupervised. Because it's a play, and you can let those parts of you out when it's a play. Our scenes together were like strange little trysts for these inner elves, like we were letting them meet at a roadside motel to get together and cackle.

We connected. It bled into our little bubble life around the show. In our dressing room filled with her cough drops and my crumpled thongs, we made each other snort laughing, hiding behind racks of clothes to scare each other between entrances, behaving like evil twins trying to sabotage the school play. There was the night that she forgot to plug her curlers in. Where her hair had been in tight tendrils for *hundreds* of entrances before, that night I looked up and saw her hair flat like an Irish setter's, blowing limp in the bad air-conditioning. Because your brain malfunctions when one tiny thing is different in a play, I thought it was the fucking funniest thing I'd ever seen. I lost oxygen knowing that she was sending me secret messages saying, *Don't you dare fucking laugh right now,* of course the funniest thing that can happen. I stared teary knives at her shoes, shaking, chewing off my tongue. She glared at the rafters swaying; we were both aware eye contact would kill us. It ruined the scene. Our inner elves backflipped with victory.

She was appalled that I was a *Pride and Prejudice* girl and had never read *Jane Eyre,* a book she read every year, and so we read it together. Her delight at my reactions to plot turns she'd been through thousands of times felt like I was reading it for the thousandth time, too, wanting desperately to give her the surrogate experience of reading her favorite book anew, because I loved her so much. I still copy her method of falling asleep when you're restless—I pretend I'm Jane, rain-soaked and hopeless in a field, with no ounce of strength left, laying my head down on a rock and giving up on the world.

Of all the lost people, even the ones I thought for the length of a van ride or confusing three days that I was in love with, Carol was my biggest heartbreak. The kinship was too eerie, the inner elves too identical. But as my dad warned with a faraway look the day after closing a production of *Hay Fever,* it is a business of saying goodbye to people. And like the other clowns, I am bad at the part when the pageantry is over, and you have to work to stay connected. Something happens when the playing pretend part is done. There are cards and hugs and hands gripping shoulders, and eye contact promises are made . . . but you know it's over. That magic open channel into the other person's hidden self is sealed over and not yours anymore.

Toward the end of the play's long run, Carol and I splurged on a shared cab back to our neighborhood. True to form we were weaving in and out of giggling and telling each other things no one knew. Or at least, the things we only gave other people who had been granted the code. Outside the cab, Manhattan went from packed Times Square to austere women in trenches with baguettes to loud and strange and wonderful Harlem. I watched Carol watch the passing city in the rain, where she'd lived and performed since before I was born. We sighed together at how much we loved it. She asked where in the city I had been on 9/11.

"Oh I wasn't here yet, I was a sophomore in high school."

A weird silence filled the cab that hadn't been there since our first pre-soul-recognition stumble through small talk. She closed her eyes tight and smiled a smile that made me sick. It reminded me of King Triton in *The Little Mermaid* right before he grants Ariel legs, thereby releasing her from his life. Or when in *Swan Lake* the coming of dawn signals the spell is fading.

". . . Betty."

She fogged the window with her mezzanine-trained breath.

"I forgot. I forgot how young you are."

I'm sure I made a stupid joke after that, but we rode the rest of the way in silence, watching the rain clean our dirty city.

The bubble was popped. We had ruined the friend-affair by doing the thing you're not supposed to do: mentioning the wife, or the existence of *return* tickets from Vegas; naming the truth that we weren't going to work on the outside. That once we weren't forced together for magic-puppet camp, we would be over. Doing this job together did all the work for us that we couldn't do ourselves. A job tells you when and where and how to be close, how to let the world fall away for the shared elves to roam. Once that pretense is gone, accessing that part of yourself on behalf of elf communion with someone whom you otherwise don't know very well would be inappropriate. And what do a twenty-four-year-old stoned slut and a sixty-seven-year old quilter . . . *do* on a platonic date?

Maybe I'm projecting too much of my real-world social impotence onto her, and any other person I've had this connection with. I think I tell myself that's it's a mutual understanding that once the play or film or whatever is over, then the spell breaks. But maybe I'm the only one putting a wall up and shrinking back once it's over. Maybe I vampire the hit of connection and then run away, afraid that I'll just disappoint them with my inability to plan brunch or text back on time. So I disappear. I rip off the Band-Aid of disappointment outright. It's too hard to stay soul-fused in the real world.

Maybe *I* am the abuser, using acting and the world around it like a little sky gondola into your soul to come spend a few weeks there. But then I have to leave, because it's not how the world works. A Cinderella where 12:01 means our eczema and taxes and spouses show up needing creams and answers about drywall.

You can spend your life chasing The Thing, weaving in and out of these types of connections, falling in and out of elf-love. There is no limit on how many times the heart can break. It is an easy addiction, easy to blink awake after a decade and see that in chasing it you forgot to water your own life. You can realize too late that during all these separate islands of fantasy time, you were *one* through-line person all along, needing vitamins and stability. I tell myself I have found a version of it that is both cathartic and healthy. But maybe that's a lie. Like when I used to eat an apple after a cigarette to "cancel out" the poison.

I am much more careful with connection than I used to be. I have learned to separate what is an unhelpful drug from what is a profound gateway. Too much naming of The Thing transforms the latter to the former. It's too beautiful and dangerous and slippery of a feeling to try to control. Feeling so invisible, and then, suddenly, seeing someone seeing you. It's a deer in the woods—just breathe through the presence of something almost holy that's about to disappear. When I feel the ice laser, when I sense elf-recognition, I try to keep the channel open without needing the other person's assurance that it's happening for them, too. I bite my tongue and let it be an unspoken little poem string that connects us. And when it dissolves, to say nothing except goodbye.

After spending a sad, stoned four years in the stained-khaki cult-camp that was boarding school, I came home. As suspected, my room was still frozen like a Pompeii tableau as thirteen-year-old me. Magazine cutouts of the Goo Goo Dolls wilted in horror at my futile attempts at the masturbation techniques the varsity hockey Sarahs had bark-taught us on a Sarah's futon between dip spits. I still had my dollhouse. I could remember its elaborate soap plot my mother and I had thought up, before this regrettable time in life where we almost hated each other. Now in life-calendar sadism, we were simultaneously experiencing the dueling Fuck Offs of menopause and seventeen. Where we had been mischief allies, we were now fist-clenched *sweet jesus not today* enemies. I'd slam the door like a trusty signature. My abandoned Barbies slurred their judgments at my ceiling-scoffs, looking like a tornado had hit their meth-themed bachelorette party.

I am half-WASP, so naturally my room had piles of crap that narcissism and laziness forbade getting rid of, and the occasional engraved silver thing under trash. An oil painting of my eight-year-old self avoided eye contact, embarrassed not only to be next to a lipstick-covered *Titanic* Leo but also to be perpetuating the family ruse that we still lived in the now-dead chapter of America where people got towels monogrammed and portraits done. Under this an ancient, framed fish had a pull-string music box feature, offering a stroke-y rendition of "As Time Goes By." I am also half–Irish Catholic, so, you know, tears in the journal and breakfast on the clothes, but also cheap whimsical novelty items peppered throughout the house to remind you life was a quick joke. (To brush one's hair or smile at the mirror would be an act of self-righteous treason, but we can make a funeral really funny.) Throughout the house, ornately framed black-and-white photos of Kennedy-looking, buzzed Virginians far outnumbered the rare blurred Polaroids of small redheaded Baltimore Christmases. The people in fox fur cheers-ing the camera could be googled—Gary Cooper once played the one with the medals and the downfall. The people in the Polaroids I knew less about.

I spent the first week home staring at these hallway pictures high as balls in orca-sized hoodies, a pointless effort to hide the obvious truth that for every year I'd been away I'd fed myself about one strand of spaghetti and a raisin. I sat emo-smoking on the roof outside my window, writing poetry that I pray to God has since been burned and the ashes sent to Jupiter. OK fuck it, for instance, this:

> *I've got too much baggage and too small a trunk*
> *I'm only telling you this 'cause I'm drunk*
> *Am I beautiful . . . now?*

Sorry.

I snaked my shitty Saab through the New England hills surrounding our house, believing the four billion Camel Lights butts I threw out the window would simply evaporate like lost socks. I'd stare at the ceiling and finally fall asleep to the fox-hunt hounds yelping across the valley, also bred for a different time and embarrassed to be there.

K. I was still sad. Looks like it was not a phase. What I had thought was indigestion in sixth grade evolved to be the Chernobyl dumpster filled with poison glue ink that replaced my organs, the razor wire hand reaching up through my throat once an hour and yanking my brain to a death basement, the thick film of *not-here* that coated the whole world. Depression! Whether it was passed down from the Tweed Smugs or the Shamrocky Repressors I don't know, but I had it bad, and at seventeen I couldn't name or control it. Now I was home and on watch. All I knew to do was quietly smoke as much weed as humanly possible and try to remember to eat so I wouldn't be subject to another profoundly embarrassing family intervention as if we knew each other that way. My parents were wonderful, but wouldn't we all rather get through family dinner without looking up each other's kumbaya skirt since we'd all just leave the table horrified anyway. The kitchen calendar told me this summer was going to feel like one trillion *Ben-Hur*s long, so I knew I had to get out of the house before I purposely concussed myself with an ancestor's horse trophy.

My boarding school friends were home far away in various Floridas and Denvers. Bunny and I were not speaking anymore. Some nights I wondered if driving fifteen minutes to her with a Camel Light and an apology would feel nice, but I never did. I knew a few kids in town from my two years of local public elementary school. I had a local best friend, Margot, who had gone away for a few years, too, but had stayed long enough to know where the parties and the drugs were so we drove around looking for both. When we rolled up to whatever land-preserve campsite or parent-less house was hosting alcohol poisoning that night, drunk kids sunburned from a day's work waved *hi* to Margot and squinted in confusion at me, some eventually remembering me from being nine, or at least pretending to.

I slowly earned my keg party keep by having a reputation for always being stoned and never drunk. I was curating an identity as a Phish fan who makes one joke and apology an hour and is otherwise silent, too afraid to be drunk and loud. So by deranged teen math I was a reliable designated driver, not that everyone wasn't driving drunk anyway. But I'd pile as many as could fit in my mushroom-stickered car interior to try to buy acceptance. I liked them and wanted in. Most of the girls were not thrilled with my showing up in slutty toddler clothes with sarcasm and red eyes at cornfield parties they'd worked for years, so most of my friends ended up being boys. And one of them was him.

Max was part Bob Dylan part Peter Pan, if Peter taught Wendy to fly with shouting and bourbon. He was Pigpen, too, covered in car and woods and whatever was around. They were all wild, but Max was a cut above, a Sid Vicious Huck Finn, living on an impressive plane of *fuck you*. I can see him weaving around a bonfire throwing his shoes in the flames and then mine for good measure. I first heard the Disney chirps of love when he punched someone in the throat and they threw up on him and then he laughed until he couldn't breathe, holding the cheeks of the victim like they were newlyweds. Weakened with joy, Max lay on the ground for the rest of the party accepting visitors like a dying

king, spitting beer in thanks at those who came to pay their re-
spects. He was a hero. And he hated me.

Early in the summer I somehow got the courage to invite myself to his house. After six Arnold-portion bong hits I announced
we would play hide-and-seek, found his at-a-sleepover sister's
bed, and waited for him. He leaned in the doorway and laughed
at me. Then he reached for my wrist. In a weird, slow, grotesque,
and somehow disturbingly hot mime, he pretended to snap off
my hand like a lobster claw. He coughed into my face. After I
didn't flinch or protest or ask why, he smiled. I had passed. He
kissed me. It was like that always—with every tenderness there
was this underlying small *I hate you. Here you go. I hate you.*

I spent most every night at his house after that—well, every
2:00 to 5:00 a.m. To earn that window I had to participate in
the kind of obstacle course that TV Pomeranians scuttle through,
if instead of hoops and tubes it was performance and loneliness, and the Muppet spinster trainer jogging me through the
course was drugs. Somewhere along the line we established a
silent code that we were not to touch in public or be perceived as
people who loved each other. I think we were both sure we were
on completely different pages: Why risk embarrassment with
naming it? We would spend parties at opposite ends of a meadow
or basement, erasing accidental eye contact by moving even farther apart or perhaps leaving without saying goodbye.

During the day he and his friends all worked, so I worked, too.
Margot and I gardened at the third-home colonial palaces that
were rapidly suffocating the county. I waited tables for the people
in pastels and boat shoes who knew my parents, their hugs completely blowing my cover of whatever I was trying to be. I had

a vague character I was playing, a sort of Eeyore Lohan Joplin, snark and smoke in a miniskirt. Bronzer and hemp to disguise the child. (You know. 2003.) At 10:00 p.m. every night my dolls and Destiny's Child cutouts watched me dress up in my Atlantic City preschool prostitute finest, in sequined napkin shirts and "skirts" that begged every chair I sat on for HPV. I was still wallflower-y in my brain but by this point had learned that a push-up bra and feigned depth could buy acceptance. I was no longer Invisible Lemur Assistant, not yet Shrugging Marilyn, but somewhere in the vague space between. Shoulders still hunched in apology over tits that were now getting huge despite my never touching protein. Ribs 'n' tits, speaking first for me before any mumbled pun could. I panic-plucked my eyebrows until they were flaccid ellipses, my old horse ribbons framing the mirror limp in disappointed snobbery. I'd pull the orca sweatshirt over it all and wave a cheery goodbye to my parents, perpetuating the lie that I was dressed for the weather and off at a reasonable hour to commune with people who cared if I lived or died. Then I'd park at the one gas station with cell phone service, sometimes for hours, chain-smoking and praying that a text from Max with instructions or clues would come through any minute. There was no way my parents would let me *leave* the house at the hour I was usually summoned, so the Mobil station was my office of pathetic girl-why-though. Why does it take us so long to ask the question, *Wait, is this hurting me?*

It was nice when we were alone. I'd lived in the country for most of my life but had never thought to spend so much time outside. Most free days he and I were in the woods just walking around being quiet, smoking and stopping to diagnose whatever haunty sound was cracking far away. There was an abandoned nineteenth-century iron mine that tunneled seemingly miles deep into the mountain, blowing freezing air onto our hallucinating sweating faces if we stood in the exact right place. I watched him pick up litter and fallen birds, jealous that the world got his sweetness and I got Hyde.

But sometimes he would stop in the trail and look back at me, or stop the car in the middle of the road and put a bizarre thumb against my eyelid, and once in a while make the ever rare, highly coveted admission that he loved me.

It's taken thirty-five years for me to realize that stopping and wondering aloud what *you* want your life to look like isn't unleashing bear spray in a nursing home. It's just what you're supposed to do. Girlhood fucks you in this way. It's hard to learn to dream when you've spent all your energy trying to *be* one for someone else.

I tried so hard to be Max's. I spent a few years following him around, coming back from college every weekend and break to sit in full ho-regalia watching his video games and fistfights, exuding at all costs how *cool with it all* I was. He would disappear at random in a terrifying *try to fucking find me* gauntlet, so I drove high through blizzards looking for him, willing to trade hours of "fuck off, fuck you" for one slurred "you're beautiful" before he passed out and I was alone with Shark Week. Then I'd drive the three-cigarettes-length ride back home, singing tearily into the tape recorder I kept in my center console, trying to convince myself I was directing this music video and not drowning.

Therapy fodder but . . . it was awful and also great. After years of beating back and farcing away the thing behind the door, the Exorcist Poe fog person leaning all their weight to infiltrate my Tuesday, it felt sort of nice to just give up and let it come have tea. And while Max and I were violent opposites, we shared this *treading water above the evil* thing. We used each other as an excuse to stop swimming for a few hours a night and let it take us. Most of our brainpeople hated each other, screaming and bailing water to get away. But one in me and one in him stared, reaching for the other across whatever basement kegger, then finally collapsing into each other in secret, happy for the first time in life to have a mirror and ally. I had had brain-twins before but never with *this* part of me, the inner Yikes. I think all our friends were profoundly confused at the match, perplexed at the rules and what it was we talked about, which sober was not a whole lot. I was a nervous priss posing as a sedated rebel. But he was the first person I loved who lived like me, making fart jokes and howling while keeping a constant foot in the black river of *we're gonna die.* I was out of my league and in over my head and also just finally home. We confuse recognition with safety again and again.

His hands were the color of the dirt he worked with all day, and I once got poison oak from him holding me after a day of clearing rich people's property. When it was too cold to be outside, we all packed the one bar in town named for George Washington— legend held the man himself once passed out drunk in that very building. Graves of pilgrims watched us all have sex and scream at each other against our cars and gaped with us in tipsy quiet at the glitter jam schmear of stars across the sky that if you saw in a movie you'd think was fake. The lookouts we'd hike to and stare out from bloodshot and giggling permanently ruined all travel for me, as I was unable to find anything nearly as beautiful ever anywhere. The roads named for the Native American chiefs and the colonists who killed them were dirt and tangled and perfect for riding eight to a car blasting Creedence en route to the party then solo home, sobbing by yourself to Chapman.

Eventually it got too lonely and confusing. At first, freshman year of college had me sprinting north to him every weekend, but then a day after acting class, when the gayest boy in overalls and a flower crown and I traded smoothies and simultaneously said in *the same* gremlin voice, "I like mine better," I knew I was finding a different kind of sameness that didn't make me also want to be dead.

I assumed Max would be elated to be rid of me, as that was the clear thesis I had received for hundreds of nights. When I called him to set him free of the curse of being mine, I was shocked to hear an unfamiliar boy on the phone, leaves crunching under his shuffling feet. In a tiny voice he told me he was terrified to lose me. Wasn't it obvious?

"I love you. I'll love you forever. You're . . . the princess."

Silence ate forty seconds. I was oxygenless. With so much instability in the relationship I had been sure of only one thing: at the end of the day he thought I was disgusting. I didn't understand then and I only sort of do now. I had been filtering and posing and suffocating—but holy shit, so had he. I thought I was disgusting so I assumed he thought it, too. Now in his cracking "wait" I realized, oh God. The same is true for him. Boys are in prison of this horrific society, too. Be the Punching Grunter Don't Cry does the same thing as Be the Laughing Nodder Don't Object. You are not asking yourself the question *Is this hurting me?*

So we had to stop. We met up on Christmas Eve and stared into the frozen river, trembling with the weight of having to actually talk. I think we ate mushrooms, desperate for something else to do besides say goodbye.

I had vastly misjudged the time and arrived home to muffled upstairs voices. The lilt and projection of my mom's tone told me it was verse. Right, of course. They were in my then eleven-year-old brother's room reading "'Twas the Night Before Christmas." Probably in unsettling slow motion, I crawled upstairs, seeing shapes in the carpet. I breathed skyward to conjure sobriety then suddenly blinked into eye contact with a stairwell Polaroid.

Mary. My mother's sister, whom I had one flash memory of meeting in a nursing home before she died. She had Down syndrome and endless faith in the world, and unwavering love for all the things in it. My brothers and I were named for my dad's horse ribbons 'n' highballs side of the family. But my middle name, Folan, was our one generational nod to my mom's Connemara and Baltimore roots. I stared up at Mary. She was my mom's favorite person and that's all I really knew. I did know that Mary's soul didn't get the chance it deserved. I also knew that the last thing she did was pretend. That every second she was just wholly and exquisitely herself. She looked at me now through frame glass with a deadpan harrumph, confused at how her niece with every privilege could waste it on misery.

A sudden inhale punched a realization into my brain. More than water or oxygen, I needed something. I needed my mom. Still tripping balls, I gripped the banister like it was a rope from a rescue copter and pulled myself to the second floor. In my brother's doorway I took in my family, huddled in pajamas and bathrobes in ministry to Claus. My brother Sam waved me in, and Harry patted the Red Sox comforter next to him. I am heartbroken now to think that I had two best friends living in the house I couldn't drive away from fast enough.

I shuffled across the floor to Harry's bed. After a few moments' debate I put my head on my mother's lap, her whole body flinching in surprise before she put her hand on my hair and continued on about the *such-a-clatter*. I thought of the Polaroids in the hallway and of Norman Rockwell paintings and wondered if the people in either of them ever felt like this.

A year later in Moscow on a school trip, I saw a sculpture of a pair of kids, the girl looking up mid-daydream and the boy she held leaning at her, wincing, letting all the black tar of the world flood in as payment for the brief excruciating bliss of admitting he loved her. I pictured him looking away and moments later without him knowing, her turning her face to him to do the same. Maybe if they had just looked at the same time it would have been different. Nicer at least. Shaking, I searched the small plaque for the title. "Rural Love."

NINETEEN

You know what's fun? *Ocean's 11*. Watching Brad Pitt be sleepy with a secret and an orange is most pleasing. Then someone else enters in a linen pant and is also tired with a secret and this time? Nachos. Last-minute nachos, you're sure of it, because it feels like you're there. You *know* this sated millionaire mused right before action, *Wait—what if I had nachos?* You feel like you are at the craft services table *with* them, advising Cheadle how to best revenge-prank Clooney. The lines and plot are sort of an adorable side-favor they're doing us—little memorized gifts for us between Zillow villa searches. No one is afraid. No one is crying. No one hates their neck. I giggle-sigh into my cereal.

Through *his* nachos, Mr. G told me the morning before opening night of *Hamlet* that I was a good actor from the neck up. "And then . . . the rest? One feels . . . sad." I went to shrug and realized I was already doing so, as my frozen posture in high school was shoulders-as-earrings. I would get dizzy in the part where I stood up fast from Ophelia's grave, making blurry the sleeping lacrosse players in the front row. My body's presence was a horrific inconvenience as an actor. It stood in the way of everything good. I did not eat, not because I cared about how I looked in jeans, but because I did not want to think about how I looked in jeans or myself at all, in any pant or town or planet.

I watched movies and was confused. The actors seemed to have zero brainpeople telling them *Stop, wait. Was that OK? Sh, self—that one was bad.* Instead they all felt oozy and free, not panicking that the boom operator hated them or that their elbows were abominations. It didn't appear that they had to slash through gluethorns of self-hate to be good in a scene, to access only every five lines the bubble of magic they had furiously dream-journaled about the night before. They did not ask, *If I disappeared would that help the story?* Instead they asked, *What if I had nachos?* My monologues were amazing to the shower curtain then terrible to footlights. I had all these ideas but so much noise in the way. I had spent my life watching people and I wanted to be them now in pretend. I wanted to show my work. I wanted to put the dark and silly into something useful to see. But one ear and eye were always pointed in, ready to berate my attempt at alchemy. I wished for anti-self-hate creativity Viagra.

I had married art with sadness. Sure, my depression was like living with a buffalo-carcass necklace, but it meant constant access to my full capacity, didn't it? A taped-open trapdoor? Wasn't hating myself the toll for being good in a scene? Inconveniently . . . no. Apparently success required the thing I didn't have: *liking yourself.* Liking yourself enough to disable self-criticism. My favorite kind of art is when someone tries their dark, silly, weird ideas. Those ideas will die in you if the loudest idea in your brain is: I should shut up.

I needed to deprogram that shit.

———

I went to theatre school. I almost went to NYU, but Anthony Moretti had gone the year before. If you remember the plot of *Felicity,* she follows a boy who doesn't love her to NYU. I didn't have the hair volume or emotional stomach to be Felicity. I went instead to Fordham. My dorm stood on what had been the fenced asphalt where the Jets and Sharks danced the opening scene of *West Side Story,* a scene I sometimes YouTube at work to trick my heart into opening on days it wants to stay closed.

If I was looking for a place to harvest weird, I certainly picked the right place. The curriculum appeared to be how strange can your day be before you raise your hand and say, *Guys? I'm out.* We writhed on the floor as electric maggots and bones-less aliens for months before we were deemed ready for dialogue. We partnered up and placed our hands on each other's tailbones and simultaneously spake monologues into each others' faces, then exchanged feedback about how their verse resonated in the bowels. We studied theatre of the absurd almost exclusively, eighteen-year-olds hunching backs and bulging eyes, snotting and screeching and hobbling around glow-tape-flecked wood floors. There was an exercise called "Nothing"—God, just typing it sends a laser-chill through my hands. You sat in a chair in front of the class and said the word "nothing." The assignment was, say "nothing" *with nothing.* You don't get it? Go to *hell.*

Meghan from Indiana sat in the chair.

"Nothi—"

"Still something." Our teacher blowdarted the word from the back. Her discerning squint was so discerning that we never knew really if her eyes were open or closed.

"Noth—"

"Mm." Squint sighed, pained.

"N—"

"—m."

Something, we nodded, we were sure of it. Poor Meghan.

The Ailey School of dance was a few blocks away, a glass tower of exploding talent. Many of its students took their academic classes with us, some sort of school partnership I was still too perma-stoned to ask about. Some of the Ailey students came to see our "Movement final." The best dancers in the world (in the *WORLD*) watched us jerk and flail and pound our pelvises sobbing into walls. One tableau made the meaningful, obvious-if-you-think-about-it tie between stripper culture and 9/11. Again, if you don't get it, I actually just feel sorry for you. Nothing. Something.

There were many moments where I looked around and thought, *Wow, cool robbery.* Charging tuition for adults to behave like hallucinating toddlers. It doesn't make sense. And then there were other moments, albeit some ten years after graduating, where I thought, *Thank God.* Because the noise in my brain was deafening. I had weirdness and thought and power in there somewhere, but the *stop* and *wait* and *hide* was so much louder. In theatre school I saw that of course this feeling was not unique, that my classmates and Matt Damon felt it, too. The distracting buzz of *shush, soul. Too loud, too dumb, not now.* It's watching someone push an idea *through* that feeling that makes you feel like you're sitting in forbidden communion with them. I saw theatre wasn't just sequined escape, it was naked examination. I had thought acting meant disconnecting from the things I hated to achieve transformation. In school I learned to use *those very things* as the medium. Make your demons trade knives for paintbrushes. And like yourself enough to do it out loud.

College was a blessed epoch of protection. We were allowed to fail for free. We took big swings with no employer or internet saying, *That was bad, you are exiled.* School was mostly gay men and brassy women bubbling with relief to find each other after being sad sore thumbs in high school. Since our syllabus was all trying-on-selves, I dropped some of the scramble in real life. I played big pulsing wild characters. Accents and eyebrows and claws, oh my!

All of a sudden, tits. This is when the ultimate plot twist, second puberty, ambushed me in the night. Physically I went from shivering Bieber to colonial Marilyn, thirty pounds of curves in two years. My cup size soared from B to . . . a letter that costume designers now blink in a pause after I say it, as if I had told them, *My bra size is gopher.* Protein and vegetables and M&M's had entered the picture. I don't know why. Maybe my brain was too bustling to remember to starve. Maybe because I was around a bunch of gay men who I wasn't posing for—who pointed to Bette Davis and Unstable-Sophomore-Corrine performing her sloth-monologue as women to celebrate. Women who dipped into the terrifying with wild eyes and full stomachs because you need a full stomach to have wild eyes. *Let's take care of ourselves so we can be sufficiently insane for the big moment in act 2.* I got boobs and hips and no one cared. Theatre was about the now and the gross. Our days were bagels and mime-orgies.

My parents came to take me out to lunch in New York as parents do. It's unclear to me now whether it was last minute or my perpetually high sophomore brain forgot the plan. I do remember the nightmare timing of a six-foot-tall bong hit and my

Motorola Razr dinging with Mom's "Where are you?" Somehow my bleary-eyed where's-my-keys self stumbled from my dorm in pajamas to a nearby Greek diner where my foot-tapping parents were waiting. My dad waved me over as he always does in calm social meetups: like he's on board the rescue ship picking up *Titanic* survivors and the sun is setting and you're the last one allowed but he's not happy about it. I wolfed down a totem pole of chocolate chip pancakes. Only once the last of the syrup was licked from the plate did I look up and ask, "Why are you dressed up?" I knew my dad's red tie and my mom's mothy heart cardigan meant an event. *Oh God,* I thought. *Did someone die and I forgot, am I about to go to a funeral stoned out of my mind?* My dad did his signature throat clear, which means, I'm about to speak, here's a pause and a breath, it's going to be important, here comes the sentence.

"As I said on the phone, your mother and I have an audition, for the same movie. In an hour. Which is why we had to be on a schedule." I briefly wondered how late I'd been and decided best not to dwell on the boring.

Then came this:

". . . You know, actually, there's a part *you're* right f—"

Out of my mouth tumbled "I'm coming with you. Give me fifteen minutes."

A new trait I noticed when I was stoned was courage. I mean, not now; now pot makes me Boo Radley inside my own skin, but then it was a sort of superpower. I sprinted back to my dorm to get ready. Years of watching my mother's backstage quick changes was my sartorial Jedi training for this moment. In fifteen minutes I was back in the diner, dressed for the role: a disapproving seventeen-year-old trailer resident. Uninvited, I went with them to the casting office. Uninvited, I wrote my name on the sign-in sheet. Marijuana and agony have since erased much of my hippocampus, but I guess I must have stolen audition sides from the trash and quickly looked over them? Again, the brazen confidence of someone whose drugs are working. My dad went in, his perfect diction booming through the door, then my mom, finding laugh lines where there were none. Then me. I don't remember being called out on my stowaway marionette status, but then this was a bizarre phase in life when I didn't commit to stone-memory every social failure. They could very well have said, *You are an unwelcome trollop,* and I could have responded, *Oh, New York,* not understanding the statement.

I got the part. Which wasn't allowed, really. They called my *parents'* home phone to try to reach *me,* saying, "We want to cast . . . your daughter," which now I wonder if my parents had a good laugh at and flipped off the phone together. But I was still a sophomore at Fordham, and I had promised my parents I'd graduate before attempting a SAG card. Fordham's rule was sort of that, too, but I was low on both parties' priority list and was just quietly allowed. I had to drop out of a school musical four days before they opened, which there was a lot of sobbing in hallways about, and impassioned emails begging forgiveness. Telenovelas have nothing on theatre school. (Would like to take this opportunity to again beg forgiveness to the cast of *Eating Out.*)

The movie was what I now understand to be a mouse-budget indie, about people being disappointed in each other in the winter. It filmed in upstate New York in February's frozen colon. The glutton level of snow everywhere looked like a joke, like we were Bahamians parodying Norman Rockwell. But I stepped off the frigid bus ecstatic, ready to emote for five dollars and my first IMDb credit.

Then I met the guy who played my brother.

We looked a little alike. His eyes were like earrings they were so far apart, and an almost stupid blue, like a computer joke. He was nine years older than me and was on fire scalding hot insane holy shit levels of my type. Meaning vibe-wise he seemed a half-asleep fireman with a sedated kitten in one hand and a swinging hammer in the other. When I saw him deep-breathe through rage at a tangled shoelace, I thought, *Oh no, we're going to have sex.* I know I said earlier don't have sex with a costar, but I'd like to amend that and say sometimes you should have sex with your costar. Jupiter is big and important, and you are small and who cares.

I shrug-skipped into a fling. My love life was an uncomfortable Jenga tower of wrong at that point. Perhaps if I had stopped to zoom out on my male interactions, I might wonder if I was a sole person or rather an asshole and victim inside a grumbling chameleon. But one doesn't zoom out at nineteen, so I was happy to add this hippie caveman to the seizing roster. During filming I settled into a routine. By day I scoffed on camera. By night, I put on my least feminist costume and trotted through snow over to Room 28. I eagerly await my Originality Award for First Actress to Conduct Trashy Obvious Showmance Because Excited Is Getting SAG Card and Thinks Invented Both Concepts.

Somehow through this movie that went nowhere, I got an agent. Thus began the decades-long Soviet beauty pageant of trying to be a professional actress. While attempting to complete my already bong-neglected college requirements, I frantically jumped through requisite New York actor hoops. I was a dead body on *Law and Order,* then months later an alive crack addict on that same *Law and Order,* an exasperated lesbian on a different *Law and Order,* then a statutory predator on the remaining *Law and Order.*

While my theatre education from my parents and school had helpfully cultivated a chasm of strange ideas, it had not prepared me for the curling iron and carry-the-one side of being an actress. To be good in a part you had to *get* a part. I learned quickly that gravitas equaled old, unsculpted hair equaled rude, choices equaled brazen. I auditioned for (the original) *Gossip Girl* to play one of the high school students and was called back for the older teacher. I was younger than the people who ended up playing the teens. But I played the audition scene as I'd been trained to—as a disturbed, scarred woman staring at the horizon with split ends and a past. What had earned me a standing ovation in Intro to Mime earned me a "next" in the real world. The punctuation-less, uncapitalized half-sentence emails I would get from my first agent with "feedback" from my first auditions made me cry every time. I was used to the hand-over-heart kid-gloved paragraphs of validation from my acting teachers. Now came gutting responses of "does she own blush?" and "unflattering face in death scene." (Really.) I'd return with more blush and less faces.

Because I wanted so lamely badly to be an actor.

Yes, because I wanted the fizzy, transcendent feeling that I grew up watching my parents grab the tail of and whisper to a few times a year. The spell of the joy and mystery of recognition that can happen, watching regional Shakespeare when you're not even sure what they're saying but for a second you feel like your soul is on trial, or a terrible commercial that's making you sob and you're not sure why. It can all be *so* bad. It can also be beautiful. I wanted to do all of that for a living.

Ambition was an alpha feeling, something I didn't recognize, but OK wow, apparently I had it. But I also had the other thing that could ruin everything.

With no proof whatsoever, just somehow knowing as 1,000 percent fact—I come from a long line of women who stayed in bed all day. Or who dreamed about it when society forced them to a luncheon or crop event. I can see in the pictures of the women on either side of my parentage that their eyes were searing *fuck this* into the camera, both in the fun-wink and the yikes-Reaper ways. I've always had a little postpartum sheen to my style, a little matted tangle and stained Henley for your nerve. There is a constant low voice encouraging me to untie the raft and drift out to sea. To float through space braless, the day's only assignment pretzels, porn, and regret. *Making the bed and having ambitions are for vain coke addicts. Listen to my voice. You are getting very sleepy.*

I told myself I had ten years to try to kill this voice. Maybe success would kill it, or some found better self, if I ran fast enough. If I couldn't do it in that time, oh well, we tried. And maybe having tried would be enough comfort when one day I would inevitably hide unmoisturized under mildewed quilts, skipping the PTA meeting because I couldn't face the women who brushed their hair.

Ironically, I began a career playing women who brushed their hair and made the bed, pulsing vanity shaking their fingers as they tucked in the sheet corners. When no one hired brown-haired, sleeve-pulling I Swear I'm a Hippie Wallflower me, I dyed my hair blond and started wearing tight Ahem I've Entered the Room clothes to auditions. I played the alphas I had studied as their trusty beta. The women whose Goodwill pile I'd sifted through as a kid, women whose accomplishments I rolled my eyes at in magazines, whose self-worth I wrote off as self-obsession. I was a proud feminist. But let's be real, *she* is unbearable. And *her*. Oy and *her*. Yay women! Except her.

Of course, it was all just me. Just me hating me. Me afraid of me.

The heartbreaking beer goggles of internalized misogyny. This combined with my Irish roots of shame and self-sabotage threatened to slash the tires of whatever future darkness getaway car I told myself I was driving. It affected my work, too. I wanted a role that accessed the basest parts of me, to have a moment on screen where I was pure id, pure Salem. My version of *what if I had nachos* ease, but instead of nachos—I don't know. Sorcery?

I felt fear standing in the way of that ever happening.

My dad used to tell us, make your bed every day until you're a person who makes the bed every day. I was going to pretend to be a person who believed in themselves until it wasn't a lie anymore. I was going to outrun whatever this ancient thing was that was trying to kill me. Or at least dance while the tide was out before the ocean swallowed me whole. Resist the temptation to beat the waves to the punch and walk out there with stones in your pockets.

I was going to try.

10

A PLAY

In a way failure was salvation. It froze time so I could keep learning. Repeated failure, no and no and no, and of course the maybes that at the last minute became you know what, no. Which is, as an actor, success. For the most part, film and TV did not want me in their club. I auditioned and auditioned and auditioned, and once every hundred times was told "OK fine, a van will pick you up at 4:30 a.m. Tuesday, you can be the drunk witness, but otherwise . . . no."

The thing I did lots of was theatre. For the first sevenish years out of school my career was mostly plays. I specialized in disturbing and confusing ones in small theatres. I writhed and screamed freely as I had been taught to. I didn't think about my lashes or waistline. Theatre did not care about those things. It would be embarrassing and unproductive to care about those things. Like an astronaut saying, *Houston, we have a problem: cellulite.*

In theatre your brain is focused on bigger problems than your éclair intake or cheek dewiness. There are global, pulsing emergencies to deal with. At some point in rehearsal, you realize the play is fucking *broken*. If you don't fix it before the first preview, everyone will die. New York will explode. Art will mean nothing. There were many moments where I sat distraught with castmates in a circle of panic. Post–disastrous final dress, we would gather, catatonic. Strewn around the set of sun-dappled living room or modernist suggestion-of-schoolhouse floating in space, we clutched binders of note-ridden scripts and vocal-rest teas. We rubbed our faces in I Can't Go On. Some changed out of their costumes immediately, real-life coats zipped to the chin to project: I'm fucking *out*. Some stayed in costume, dazed, telegraphing: Change clothes? I don't even know what *hands* are anymore.

The Importance of a Play was a perfect and necessary distraction from the Importance of Me. It was as if I had been granted the pause I'd been praying for, the time to just not think about answers and instead ask four billion questions. Theatre was all about the unspoken. "Table work" was the first week of rehearsal, before actors are on their feet with their scripts and blocking scenes. You spent the first seven days reading the script seated with coffee and pauses, raising your hand with related anecdotes and pronunciation attempts. But topics like what the recurring blue light *meant* and did Cleo *really* kill the offstage kitten or was it in Cleo's mind were forbidden. Putting answers in stone was not OK. At table work when someone asked a question, often the playwright would respond after a pregnant silence, "I'd rather not say," and everyone would go, "Mm."

I did a play where obscurity was law. A play by a genius, a man whose work we studied lots of in school. Would this particular play have been produced if it were not by an accomplished famous playwright? Did this particular emperor have clothes? *I'd rather not say.* But here's what wasn't allowed in that rehearsal, ever: concrete answers, cogent narrative, subtlety. I played a mute ghost—or *was* I a ghost? Also, *was* I mute? I knew not to ask. One day the director told an actor to exit to the kitchen. "Sorry—is the kitchen stage left or right?" Silence filled the room like a toilet vapor. Someone. Had asked. A *question*. We inhaled and braced for the planet to break in half. ". . . Let's move on," the director finally breathed, ushering us toward safety. Once in rehearsal the disgruntled savant playwright himself decided to attend and watch a run-through. His note was "remember colors." "You mean, tones of a scene?" the director prompted helpfully. "No, God no. I mean red. I mean . . . purple. *Blue*." "*Mm*," I said, choking a little, the mute ghost having not spoken for the three-hour run time.

The possibly mute possibly ghost was also possibly a nurse. I think? I was in a nurse's *outfit* at least, a 1960s Hitchcock damsel attendant pushing a wheelchair. In said wheelchair was my character's master, played by an elder dame with a gravel voice and child's smile. I wheeled her around a dramatically sloped stage, her fragile and important life in my literal hands. At the confounding climax of the first act, I, in heels, had to push her up an Everest-steep ramp to an "overlook." It was meant to be a cliff, which was meant to be a metaphor. In reality it was an unstable black square of wood fifty feet in the air, jutting over an equally black abyss of audience. One slip, one sneeze, and I would be in jail for pushing a legend off a (metaphor but actual) cliff, launching her into the void of terrified and confused patrons.

She was in her eighties and had long, insane monologues that the savant kept changing daily. She paraphrased in ways I found excruciatingly hilarious, my hands covered in tiny purple half-moons from my nails digging into my flesh to stifle my illegal laugh. Searching for the text in her brain, she improvised plot points that derailed the already-nonexistent logic of the play, once offering that Miggs was dead right before Miggs entered. Sometimes she lobbed *me* a question, hoping I might help steer her back to the correct script. I felt the audience turn to me, shifting in pity that *I'd* forgotten *my* line. I did all I could do: pray that my bugged, vibrating eyes could beam the truth to this legend. *I am mute, and we're at the bottom of page 114.*

When I was a kid, I had only seen the silly and fantastical— watching my parents and their friends lace up corsets and entertain, then unlace them and talk shit. In practice I felt the other side of theatre, the constant flip between art and mortification. In the play where I met Carol, my character Elsie was a nervous lab assistant, scurrying upstage and down in pursuit of love. On the last day my Secret Santa revealed himself to be the sound-booth operator, who gave me tinseled wine in the hallway. Hand over his heart, he launched into a string of good-job-compliments, and I thought, *OK, Betty, take this in.* He listed Elsie's hidden tells of loneliness, things I'd laced in privately, wondering if anyone out there *got it.* Looks like sound guy Todd *had.* Maybe that made the four months of audiences *not* getting it worth it after all. "And my *favorite* thing about Elsie?" Defenses down, I nodded meaningfully for him to continue, teary eye contact, my hand over *my* heart now, too. He clasped my shoulder in solidarity. "Her *heartbreaking walk!*"

Now my hopeful Labrador face dropped to a drugged basset hound. I nodded a stiff thanks. It was too painful to say, *Um, that. Was uh. Just . . . just my normal walk.* We shook hands and I got on the elevator with my humidifier.

I did a play out of town at a summer theatre festival, a

two-woman show playing thirteen different characters with thirteen different costumes. The audience hated all thirteen. I didn't know, and I was in heaven. At the same festival years later, I did a play they hated even more, where I hung myself in the last scene. That time the hatred was pretty clear to me. The final thirty minutes were a monologue swinging from a noose. I spoke directly *to* the audience, a playwrighting device that should be outlawed. Direct address is especially sad when the audience is visibly asleep or in pain. Also when you're in a noose.

The noose scene was preceded by a high-stakes quick change into a "safety mechanism." I had thirty-two seconds to sprint off-stage into pitch black, take off all my clothes, pull the tangled full-body harness on over my flailing limbs, put a different costume over it, and reenter, drunk and sobbing. The karmic payback of my former stoned seventeen-year-old self came now; the quick change was done not by alert adult professionals but dazed teen interns. They pawed absently in the pitch dark at clasps and ties meant to ensure I wouldn't *actually hang myself.* "You . . . should be good" or "Wait! Eh, never mind" was often whispered to me as I John-Wayned back into the spotlight, now with the silhouette of an upright bison. Every step jangled the tell to the audience of *I'm wearing something elaborate under this sweatshirt: it's for the plot.* The drop of the noose from the rafters was supposed to elicit a huge gasping shock, but every night I felt the audience go, *Oy. Huh OK so I guess she's wearing a . . . harness? So this actress doesn't actually hang herself on my free Thursday?* Not knowing for sure if the bloodshot Mackenzies had double-checked the death-buckles, I stepped off the top rung of a ladder with a rope around my neck. I shrugged into the dark, thinking, *We'll see!*

This festival is where I met a best friend. Patrick was doing another play that was equally confounding and perfect, and in Camel Lights breaks on a bench by the theatre we fell in friend love. We played Anita and Maria in duets to the empty parking lot and YouTubed Tony performances till dawn in my room. He took my hand and told me with kindness that the magentas and Lycras that crowded my closet were not helping me. He told me he was so afraid that the director of his play was going to correct an older actor's pronunciation of "*Murray* Hill." The old man said the line putting the emphasis on the first word instead of the usual second, and Patrick didn't know why, but it made him feel *so happy.* I swallowed back embarrassing too-soon tears of "yes, yes I know *just* what you mean!" I thought of all the times in my parents' plays when the way an actor would say a particular line every night felt like a knot was untangled in my brain.

Our friendship bled back into New York. We'd go see theatre together, glaring *God when will this be over* eye contact, then clutching each other in *God let this never end* bliss. We'd laugh loud and sigh loud at all the right parts, knowing how hard it all was up there and playing *our* part from the audience. Patrick would come to plays I was in and say all the right things expertly; specific compliments for all, then five blocks away and the coast was clear, "He really doesn't *want* to choose *when* to scream, does he?"

Almost twenty years after his smile sent me for the cliff's edge, Anthony Moretti was on Broadway. As only a gay best friend could, Patrick both knew the drama of the personal stakes at hand and was off book for the musical in question. "I know he destroyed you in high school. But Betty. We're *going.* It's going to sweep the Tonys!"

In the dimming lights surrounded by the octogenarians that keep theatre alive, I suddenly panicked. Maybe Anthony would be bad, or ugly, and my life would have turned upside down from the puppy love equivalent of beer goggles. I fixed my hair in the dark.

Then suddenly in the corner of the theatre, there he was. He strummed the first chord of a song my dad and I had wailed every day together in the Volvo to daycare. Anthony breathed in a sigh that was mine for a month. (I know, fine: three fucking weeks.) He exhaled a long clear note that once sailed across the stage at me in *Kiss Me Kate,* this time ending with a toe-curling vibrato that sent a female murmur of *oh shit* across the room. Patrick started sobbing. The house stayed lit with Anthony, making audience eye contact possible. (OK, maybe not *all* direct address is illegal.) As he sauntered closer through the song, I lost my breath knowing what was coming. Anthony found my eyes with a little shrug, as if this were his plan the whole time, my life until now a little joke. He sang a few words into my face. I laughed and then just . . . shrugged back. A few seconds of Rodgers and Hammerstein forgiveness. Then the lights shifted, and he walked away. A few character actors sauntered in with harmonies that made me feel six. I grabbed my friend who loved me's hand. We sat panting in the magic.

The fucking theatre. Peppered in between all the moments of embarrassment were the best blips of ecstasy. The moments where the trick worked. These little stop-the-world pauses where the whole theatre breathed together and thought about the same thing, or realized in the same moment that the cantaloupe in the end is like the shoe in the beginning and oh God no, the lights fading means this will end, swim here in this second before it disappears. And it makes row D think about Uncle R and row A think about how they never said *x* before *y* died. Onstage you feel it, the shift in the universe that for this millisecond, it's working. A darkened audience full of brains here in this exact instant together, weaving in and out of being so deep in the story that it feels real and then that story catapulting you into a thought about your own life. Even the most terrible plays I was in had moments like this, where you thought, *It's happening, now.* It feels like when you're a kid in kid-gym and you do the group circus-parachute thing where it explodes up in the air then you all run forward and sit down, butts on the chute, creating an already deflating fort of *We're here, for a few more seconds we're here, can you believe it?* And you smile blinking at everyone in the crumpling circus, thinking this moment is now, it's now, it's now, it's gone.

11

OPTIONS ARE PARALYSIS

The bad thing about the patriarchy getting a disease where its dick slowly rots and falls off is that now we have options, and options are paralysis. A society built around gender serfdom, yes, should be lit on fire and the ashes peed on. The new society should be surrounded by statues of the severed diseased dicks as a reminder that here, no subjugation without equal castration.

But at every turn, the choose-your-own-adventure portion of freedom has me eyeing the "never mind" exit staircase before the big kids' waterslide. We are living in a time where women are refurbishing shackles as novelty earrings. We take things built to control us and treat them as optional pieces of flair. Marriage. Motherhood. Mascara. I hope ghosts of lapelled bros are tantruming in their graves, furious as we renovate the dungeons they built for us into slutty libraries and existential craft rooms.

The most obvious way to tell history to suck it as a modern wo-man is to choose a career and excel. Pause to dust the glass ceiling shards from your shoulder pads and keep soaring. Turn your passion into pension. I marvel-chew through a stoop-muffin at New York women walking *fast,* boots slapping against the pavement, making needs known on speakerphone with no pauses offered or permission asked. You type and talk and text your way into revenge for your grandmother. You run the boardroom that she was never allowed inside. I force myself to write assertive work emails and ask for what *he's* having. A life spent filling your resume and bank account will surely stick it to the ancestor who thought you were meant for doilies and submission. Or maybe it's not a career, maybe it's just living for *you*—your she-feet in Birkenstocks walking through Naples with your *two* boyfriends. Love that for you.

Perhaps when all that's done or on the side if you have time, *maybe* you pepper a wedding or a crib in there. Eventually. If you feel like it.

But also . . . ugh. I don't know. Given the actual *choice* . . . when are you going to *feel* like doing either of those terrifying illogical things?

It was simpler when you turned *x* age and just had to marry the pocketwatchy, sweating dude nearest you, then turned another age and stared at the ceiling thinking about meadows or Saturn while he grunted a bug into you so you could do literally everything else parent-wise for the rest of your life. Then maybe you read a little pearl-embossed Bible near a harp while the men discussed policy and afterlife and in the corner the next crop of femme-serfs discussed a needlepoint of a duck.

Now we don't have to do that! Your future is not a choiceless prison! Congratulations, you were born in the generation where you get to man the remote of your own fucking life!

. . . Gulp. *Y-yay!*

Sorry? Oh, I'm fine. These are tremors of . . . joy!

. . . OK yes, I'm terrified.

Speaking as someone paralyzed by decisions, I think the one perk of the gender serfdom of yore was that your destiny was not your fault. Suppression meant a choiceless iCal. No floaty she-ancestors turning to you, saying, "How will *you* do it when we could not?" No staring across a two-top wondering if his confounding pronunciation of a Portuguese wine like he's Portugal itself renders him unworthy of coitus or a prenup. No panicking if you should have fucked everyone you saw in Ecuador because Caroline did in Moscow and now you're both in Starbucks and she's winning Tuesday. No *I know it's our honeymoon, but has he always laughed like that?* Or no *oh shit I'm suddenly* x *age and no one was good enough and now single men who are also* x *age have hairless cats or murder history and I guess maybe I did want some of the picket fence stuff I spent most of my life spraying pee at as I ran.* After centuries of fighting for choice, you are the one who gets to choose. What if you choose wrong?

Listen—thank *God* we are progressing, albeit at a Xanax-ed snail's pace, toward gender equality. Profoundly embarrassing it's taken this long. I'm sure I am a dinosaur in my discomfort. I do in many ways feel like the brand of woman who will be squinted at a hundred years from now in pictures, and they'll think, *Holy shit, they still had* those *kinds then?*

I watch women around me dynamite down barricades without a lip bite of worry. And then there's me.

Presented with life choices, I find myself a shivering rodent, stalling for time, terrified to take a step. It's mortifying and archaic. My self-doubt in seizing my own life and body and timeline feels like I'm clinging to a phonograph in the class photo for Google. Or have a prehistoric tail where everyone else has robotic fins.

Already I feel women ten years younger than me seem fifty years younger, so sure and sparkling with newness of thought. They seem to be hooked up to the latest software update—biological clocks and monogamy tropes are for cancelled grandmothers.

Now there is freedom. Which means you get to choose *when*. And *who*. And *why*.

You get to choose the exact life you want.

Again: Y . . . yaaaay! *Am* I crying? I didn't think that was noticeable, sorry!

Perhaps this choose-your-life assignment is thrilling if your brain is a Pinterest board in blood of Who You Are and What You Like. If you're the friend who orders for the table, if you unpack immediately, if you've straightened a drunken frame in a home that's not yours, maybe you don't feel the fears. Maybe a blank slate on which to chisel the logistics of your life is an afternoon's bliss. But as a human tornado of Help Wanted, I think my kind overlaps with yours on one remaining patriarchal section of the test. Freedom is bliss both for passport misplacers and for color coders. But at some point we have to make the big, terrifying, deliberate, *yep-this-one-I'm-sure* life choices. First, yes, there's figuring out what kind of person you want to be. And what that person's dreams are, be it conference call or porch nap. Impossibly and simultaneously, there's something else.

Picking a person. Then maybe . . . *having* a person.

And when. And *why*.

Or if you want either of these things at all.

Suddenly freedom feels like a toddler's cement turtleneck around your female adult clavicle.

At first it's fun. *Who do I choose!* And once I choose, do I even *want* kids? But then slowly you realize we're pretending we're in the future but we're not, that dating as a (boringly straight) woman is not the woke romp of exploration that you told yourself it would be. So much of heterosexual dating is still soaked in Eisenhower-era quagmires. In early copulations, I told myself I was on an evolved quest of self. It took forever to realize I wasn't searching; I was posing. I wasn't experiencing; I was performing. I was desperate to see my fantasy self reflected in my partner's eyes, only caring about Eisenhower-approval points and not about who the person yawning into my face actually *was*. A perfect recipe for realizing too late that I was in nightmare situations.

And was that sex even *good*?

In my first forays into fucking, I was posing for most of it, believing my orgasm achievement meant I had to submit my sexual performance to his internal committee of approval. Only if everything was looking porny and going well could *I* pursue an orgasm if time permitted and it happened by accident. Meanwhile no such committee submission happened for the dudes, orgasms and Monday high fives a guarantee. No arching and curling for reassurance and bro-cameras that aren't there but could be so suck it in. Most of my early sexual experiences felt like I was a dressage horse on roller skates insisting it all Felt Great, and the He was a blind boar on ketamine who loved cocaine, in a room full of it. (My clitoris in this metaphor being an optional rice-sized light switch on the roof.)

But then eventually you have actual good sex. You are asked real questions. You try things like tapas and anal. And the billion off-ramps and side doors of your life's possibilities reveal themselves. You realize, oh thank *God,* I don't have to just choose the burping, problematic, stained-sheets guy who won't learn my middle name as a point of pride. Just because we *could* be together doesn't mean we *have* to be. This is the new dawn. I'm gone. I'm going to find and choose exactly who I want to be. And be with. And create. Then your life becomes an exciting *But with who!* game show. You are not a cow forced to trot one way through a maze toward that horrific Good Night Forever wand thing. You're the cow's descendant, standing tall with pierced udders, liberated and unsupervised in Grand Central Station.

Well? Right or left? Or up? Can't you fly?

Take my own male partner person. He is my choice, I am his choice, everything's great. The volume level of his sneeze sends me to Mars. It is an insane, rude, thousand-voweled bro-bark to the clouds, shot one naked centimeter from my eardrum. When he sneezes, I can't believe we are together. My brain goes down a billion-mile-an-hour hole of every time I've shrunk entering a room, or said *sorry* to someone who bumped into *me,* and here I've chosen a monster who thinks a sneeze is an excuse to fucking SCREAM to the world that I'm Here and Aren't I Terrifying and Important, Isn't This Sneeze *the Sneeze.* He sneezes and my face turns into a stone plate. I radiate hatred and regret. Of all the choices in the world, I have chosen this sneeze.

But I remember the First Sneeze. I remember his sneezing and my laughing so hard at it, both drunk, standing in an Upper West Side Dunkin' Donuts at 4:00 a.m., the aproned woman fetching my chocolate glaze joining me in incredulous peals of laughter. The Sneeze got that same reaction for the first few months, as if it were a trick just for me, a sort of throwing a million ribbons in the air every time he had allergies just to make me laugh.

Then Time happened.

My reaction to the Sneeze shifted to a sort of eyebrow raise and nod as if to say, *Yes, you mentioned you have a boat.* Then I slowly realized the evil truth pulsing there for years that I didn't see before. No, his Sneeze was not a shared experience of absurdist joy, howling at the gods with donuts, but a calculated plot against me. A gaslighting campaign of time-released screams to punctuate my entire life. In a world where I wear empowerment like an ill-fitting costume and then offend its name with my own tiny squirrel sneeze. In a sin against feminism, I've committed to a man who, every time he sneezes, forefathers in heaven spank their wives with one hand and high-five with the other, a chain across the sky to mock my freedom. And a version of my life passes through my brain where I chose differently, I chose a mute professor whose nose was removed in a lifesaving surgery, and when *his* body has the instinct to sneeze, he instead just signs me a compliment, because it gives him the same level of satisfaction.

I try to explain this feeling to my single friends, and fail. Part of having the gift of choice is the occasional murderous notion that you chose wrong. Even when you chose right.

I am now of an age where the option menu has changed. Now babies and marriage have replaced fisting and Paris. Modern feminism is better for the latter. A montage of looking over water and journal pages and a myriad of balls thinking, *My God, I'm Cleopatra in a romper.* It feels like the antithesis of progress to put down your telescope and pick up a breast pump. Find yourself. No, find a partner. Freedom or family?

There's only so much time to work toward both.

I wanted both.

Early on I met a man who was annoyingly different. I broke my own rule and continued seeing my showmance, the sedated fireman-looking person who had played my on-screen brother. Our early courtship was the stuff of Reasons Not to Have a Daughter. Pouring whiskey on each other in motels, my donning lime-green, velour shorts the size of a postcard and saunter- ing alone to his seventeen-subway-stops-north neighborhood, stoned at 4:00 a.m., sending texts that if published would have me banned from churches. It was perfect. It felt like the frantic *Eat Pray Kerouac* work that I *should* be doing, writing the story of my twenties that modern women were supposed to write. Wild! Whorish! Unpredictable! I was reading *The Alchemist*! In *Spanish,* bitch!

Then one day we were in his disgusting thousand-roommates- yet-no-one-cleaned bathroom. We had just gotten out of the shower, because our level of physical ho-addiction required shower- ing together. I leaned over, arching and flexing of course, to put my wet hair in a towel. I heard a familiar sound. *Bacon,* I thought, sizzling in the pan, *we should order break-fAAAAAAUUUUUUGGGGHHHH.*

My white lunar loaf of a lapsed Protestant ass pressed against the scalding-hot water pipe. The sound of bacon was a correct as- sessment as my *ass-flesh was fucking burning.* I screamed an unsexy scream and coiled in an unsexy coil. And I panicked.

In the perfect character I had crafted for this genre of my life, this plot turn did not make sense. I had this man by the emotional *balls.* For months and months, the power had been mine. Reader, I'd wear a tube top with a joint stuck in my cleavage to meet at a *museum.* I would put on mascara before he woke up. I'd disappear for days and respond to texts at a beat-poet-cool-level rate. I kept my childhood a mystery, occasionally referring to vague swaths of trauma that were none of his business. Wearing underwear was a distant dream. But this, this was a nightmare. Getting a billion-degree burn on my ass in his presence and gutturally screaming like an amputee-d sow was not the plan. It poured acid on my perfectly edited script.

For his reaction, I prepared for the usual. I had been with very different men, but one trait overlap was saying with one's mouth full of tortellini, "Oh shit, did you want pasta, too?" A general sense that when it came to taking care of each other, I was regarded as a plastic houseplant. Self-sufficient and obsolete. One guy told me "don't bother coming over when you have your period." I dated him for two years. (CEEEEL-A-BRATE GOOD TIMES *COME ON!* DADADADADA, ISSASELLABRAYSHUN)

Instead, suddenly, I was in the air. I was scooped up like a maiden who hath slipped on the ice outside church. He carried my soaking and seared body down the hall at a walking speed I hadn't thought this sedated cowboy capable of. For a moment I thought he was just going to walk me right out onto the street and toss me out like a leaking trash bag and that would be the end of us.

But no. He laid me on his bed. Suddenly I was a patient in a wizard healer's cottage. An impressive aloe plant I'd never noticed was snipped at in a hushed voice I'd never heard him use. Suddenly the ass I'd insisted was only for spanking was now skinless and horrific and fluorescent in his face. A face that was not disgusted but . . . concentrated. Kind. He applied plant salves to my leper ass for the rest of the day. He insisted I stay prone and pant-less in front of the TV; the burn had to breathe. He called his mom, a nurse, on speakerphone. He used my name without context to her, like he'd told her about me. And when he paused in the doorway to go get prescription ointment and said, "And maybe something *else*," and I knew he meant peanut M&M's, I felt sick.

Inconveniently, I fell in love with him.

Inconvenient because I was young, and I knew my modern-woman life-choices tally was nowhere near where it needed to be if I were going to submit it to my ancestors and future daughters to impress them. I still needed to fuck a Russian professor and three women and try pottery and live in Barcelona. I also needed to focus on achieving an IMDb page that would rescue me from hereditary darkdarksadsad. Any semblance of roots or permanence was for one's far-off thirties, if not forties.

He felt the same. He was nowhere near exorcising the male version of this; the demon that makes men want to take home every cocktail waitress and light Subarus on fire. We were realizing the sick truth that we could *really* be together, but both needed time to fill the solo-horizon running column before settling down. But didn't want to lose each other.

So we tried to do both.

We started an open relationship.

Which for straight people is like Abraham and Mary Todd insisting they can figure out TikTok.

A sort of "don't ask don't tell" policy was installed. But we were still so addicted to each other that we'd spend four or five nights a week together, and "who knew" where we were on the off-nights.

On one such off-night, a girlfriend pointed her Parliament at me and slurred:

"Men have been doing this for centuries. Just without permission. He's going to be better at it than you. You can't let him win. *For Bessy Ross.*"

Not sure if she eliminated the *t* on purpose or if the dollar beers did it for her, but I understood her meaning. Our femmecestors were watching. I couldn't let them down.

So I tried.

But the truth is I was still me, and men were still men. I wasn't the hardened, sex-positive, thousand-yard-stare poem I insisted I was. I mean, I had my moments. But at my core, I was still an approval-seeking, self-hating apologizer, blind to red flags and situations that hurt me if they seemed shiny at first. If New York had feminist Russian professors seeking mutually satisfying one-night stands, I didn't find them.

I did find a movie star with a serial-killer kitchen (gleaming eggshell knife museum) who told me over haggis that he didn't want to ever "do anything to diminish his sparkle." I *wish* I were exaggerating to make this book better. But he said it and I slept with him, OK? I saw clearly the character he wanted me to be, and I obediently played it. Or auditioned to play it—it never felt like I got the part. But I assumed the role of Gee Whillikers Unemployed Actress, and the script was just to be in general awe of his majesty. I treated him like he was Daniel Day Hemingway. (Even though his career canon was what your mom watches if there's nothing else on.) Once while crossing the street toward him I could feel him watching me and I pretended not to know, squinting down at the pavement pretending to have a terribly deep thought cross my brain, performing darkness for him to be curious about. When I walked up to him holding a cigarette out to me in his doorway, he laughed in my face: "You think I don't know you were faking?"

But my disappearing uptown for most of the week kept him interested, or at least annoyed I wasn't begging for his sparkle.

So he pulled out some stops. We went on a double date with a *real* genius once, a now-frail actor whom I wished I could tell my parents I had *cacio e pepe* with, but the surrounding circumstances were too dark for a Thanksgiving anecdote. The elder genius's date was a guy who I thought was my age but when we went outside to smoke a joint on Bowery together, I saw he was even younger than me. From the snow, the two of us watched through the window as an opera singer came to our table and sang to the genius, his wrinkled smile staring into his special soup that wasn't on the menu. My date puffed with pride at the hushed restaurant, believing the spectacle was also for him. The boy and I giggled, shivering at our two empty chairs, napkins folded in swans atop them, deadpan upholstery soaking up the aria, waiting for next week's replacement teenage arm candy. Musical chairs indeed.

Don't check your phone, I told myself. *It's an off-night.*

There were others, too, but not nearly as many as I let my Harlem beau believe. What I couldn't keep track of were the MEs. Wide-Eyed Ingénue Amazed at All the Cashmere, New York Priss Eats Live Crawfish to Prove Grit, Girl in Bar Who Hates You, Girl in Bar Who *Gets* You, Girl on C Train Who Wishes She Could, Costar with Same Sense of Humor and Curated Sweater Collection, and on and on.

Exhausting.

What was strange was that the boy in the North, the aloe-applying doorway-pauser, started to see through all of it. And I saw through him. Impossibly, his existence cut through my solipsism. So much of dating and career had been painting myself as an illusion, and watching someone fall for it. Or seeking out qualities in other people that existed in myself—sameness was assurance that I was worthy or important. This pursuit made me selfish and blind to the best things, things that have nothing to do with validation. True love fixes this. The curiosity of falling in love with someone finally overrides the priority that they are curious about *you.* Instead I started to wonder about him. Not how he felt about *me,* but who *he* really was. The vanity of my fear of Being Found Out had stood in the way of Being Known. And Knowing Someone. Falling in love made me forget to pretend I was some desirable mystery character. Uptown I slipped. Accidentally I was just me, Salem-y unfiltered id, perched on his futon, cackling with noodles.

We told ourselves we were evolved geniuses for keeping the relationship open, but it was mostly insane. New York is too small for anyone to lead double and triple lives. I found heterosexuality to be too insular and archaic to infuse new rules. (I hope you have had better luck.) Our friends were horrified and "caught" us both, violating our secret rules in telling the other. "I saw her on Fourteenth leaning on *x,* holding pizza," he was told. "I saw him go into a slutty Dalmatian's dorm room last night," a friend called to tell me one November 1. She was dressed as Storm from *X-Men.* Drunk in Lyrca and a cape, she had screamed at him. He once growled to the ceiling above his bed in a low voice that he wanted to kill the movie star. Another night, holding me, he said, "Oh B, you left a fancy earring in my bed!" I let the ice quiet and cheek-turn remind him that my ears weren't pierced.

Idiots.

Excruciating.

It went on for years.

If only I had an octopus fire hose and could put out all the multiple shame-fires at once, charging ahead toward jobs *and* him *and* liberation. I saw the three categories of how I was supposed to be spending my twenties—career, partner, self—and worried there would only be time to achieve one. Maybe I'd pick the wrong one and spend my gray-haired years mourning the other two. Alone in a Four Seasons for a Tokyo press tour, ringless and sexless. Or maybe married in a cabin, depressed and unemployed. Or maybe gonorrhea in a different serial-killer kitchen every month. Question for the room: How are we supposed to do this?

The tote bags and hashtags that seem to be the skywriting of modern feminism would have you believe we solved it. That we have achieved this Eden of Doing All at Once. Try out every version of your life with arms open, but also sink your feet into the earth so they turn into roots. Be a woke RV roaming the world alone for epiphanies but also be a fixed cement bunker collecting batteries and diapers. Also, be a booming business with no time to do either of these things. The totes lie. We haven't figured it out yet. Trying to find yourself *and* feed yourself simultaneously is maybe impossible.

There are stone walls all over the area I grew up in, moss-covered, zigzagging the woods—delineating property lines from hundreds of years ago. I always picture women sitting on them sobbing. Corseted and milk-stained, alone in the woods, trapped in a life they didn't choose. And I, on a hike blasting Rihanna to take my mind off business emails, walk through their ghosts like cobwebs I don't notice, tantruming about all the decisions.

12

THE PALACE THE LIGHT THE LOBBY

Yes, I wanted to be successful. But I did not mean L'Oréal deal and six Oscars or suicide. I aimed low and nonspecifically for various reasons.

One: having the exclusive goal as an actor to be rich, famous, *and* happy is . . . insane. It's delusion soup. That's like saying *I'll only be happy if a snow leopard and bald eagle both appear in my hometown the day of a rare comet, and if it doesn't happen, I'll evaporate.* Staying up late dreaming of your face on magazines and your name on the lips of all the string-pullers, of the masses falling in the perfect mix of endeared and attracted and in awe of you, all from work that was transcendent and not embarrassing, *and* all of that equaling a happy life . . . is just. Not. Fucking. Possible.

Meaning it doesn't exist.

Or when it does, it lasts for four seconds, or it feels like that for maybe fifteen minutes of that person's day, and everything around it is trying to get back to that feeling that you were secure and wanted. It is a business designed to play on your "but what's over there?" brain, every little taste of satisfaction dying on your tongue the second you register it as victory. I am *so* much further in my career than I *ever ever ever* dreamed I could approach being, and yet in darker afternoons there is a voice saying ". . . al*most, huh?*"

Whatever your thing was in the high school lunchroom, that is how you will feel in your career. Attention and paychecks don't make it better. They make it louder. At fifteen I felt invisible, hiding in the queen's shadow, too cowardly to seize something myself. The number of times I have felt this professionally is mortifying. Or rather, the number of times I have made *myself* feel this way because the brain is a liar. I hear friends describe their own careers, and I gape at the mental Cirque du So-crazy it took to get them to that conclusion. Career dysmorphia will kill us all. The only people I've heard shaking over an omelette saying, "But when will *I* be a movie star?" are . . . movie stars.

(I'm not saying happy movie stars don't exist. I'm saying the ones that are have found happiness elsewhere, around a business designed to make them *un*happy. Like living with an alcoholic grandpa, but at a strategic distance with therapy and a guesthouse.)

Well, maybe I lied before. Saying that I aimed nonspecifically maybe isn't true. It's the excruciatingly boring lesson I apparently keep having to fucking relearn: I *do* have a person in me that is pointing to Neptune and saying, "We can go there. I know how to make spacewings." A person who walks into internal utility sheds and says, "Guys, there's so much stuff we're not using." "Let's try for *that* job—why not?" "Just write down that *yes,* you can salsa, and we'll figure it out if you get the part." "Let's write a book."

This tiny brainperson has a dream that is specific and strange.

Their idea of success has more to do with victory over my own demons than public validation. The problem is that that person's voice is so soft and their cell phone connection to my brain so choppy that *any* outside wind or musing can drown it out completely.

This is where the entertainment business sidles up like Iago or Scar, and in a by turns maternal and sexy voice pours the poison into your ear of "what you *really* want." If your own Goals to Happiness are written in shaky pencil on a leaf in a tornado, the Business slides a glittering stone tablet over to you, insisting you can just copy its notes instead. *It's cute that you just want to "do good work and not be broke." Trust me, I think it's adorable. And the whole having a family and other interests thing? So fun. What if I told you that we could make the world think you were God? I see that you're resting on this level you've made it to. I totally get that you're proud to have made it this far, we were just talking about how sweet that was. What if I told you that just up those stairs, a little farther, is a palace? A palace filled with room service and compliments, and free alpaca sweatpants and novelty sneakers, and all the scripts of your favorite books begging for you to memorize them for more sneakers, and a comments section filled with the Midwest screaming in all caps that you're their queen? Wouldn't that feel nice? Doesn't that feel like a good goal? Sh sh sh, don't worry about that. We can cover that up, we can light that just right so they won't see. Sorry what? You wanted to go to Bali this summer? Mmhmm. And you're how old? No no, sorry, I'm just doing quick math and . . . yeah I feel like . . . there's not really time for Bali? Now? Let's earn Bali. Like OK, I didn't want to say this out loud but . . . there's only so much room upstairs in the palace. We're only letting like, twenty-six people in there. Out of the four hundred on this level. Which—totally congrats on getting to the four hundred! And listen, if you're fine here, we're actually . . . we're of course considering other . . . it's a competitive—you know what, actually this is my four o'clock, I should—you're canceling Bali? That's my girl.*

(Do not. Cancel. Bali. This. Voice. Is. Not. Your. Friend.)

*What? No of course I'm your friend! I'm your **dream.** It doesn't matter that it's different from what you wrote down when you were six—my version is better. And you didn't think you'd get this close to the palace then! You were just a dumb six-year-old who liked show tunes. You didn't know you'd get the chance to meet Zeus. More What? Oh ha, was that one of your obscure jokes? Yeaaah, so, I get that you're "weird." I get that that's part of what got you this far. But if you want to make it to the palace? You have to appeal to everyone. Weird is niche. Let's do a fun personality surgery where we shave off anything that's remotely alt or unique or controversial. That way you'll appeal to gallery owners **and** Pizzagate truthers. It's hard to have a negative opinion about a paper cup of sand, you know? Especially one with tits. Are you writing this down?*

What this voice doesn't tell you is that while it has your eye contact, it's pushing the leaf you wrote your *actual* dreams on closer to the fireplace. It hopes that someday you'll forget what you wrote down to begin with. The voice learns to disguise its tone to sound a lot like your own. And in that now-familiar voice you trust, it says, *Hi: you're a failure. You're running out of time. And, this goes without saying, but: you're gross.*

It wants us to forget the tiny light. That thing buried in you that is your unique, wild, only-yours gift. Focusing on unearthing *that* should be the ultimate goal. Having it float out into a room. Even if just for a moment. *Your* moment.

What I'm realizing is achieving this externalization of the tiny light has a lot fewer trumpets and metamorphoses than I thought it would. It's going to sting when the world doesn't see it as holy as you do. Especially not in the palace. Contrary to what the voice told you, no one cares about your pinprick of light there. At all. No one in the palace is going to hold you by your shoulders and read aloud to hushed cherubs what was written on your leaf. You burst through the palace doors and say, "I'm ready for soul alchemy, I'm ready for the tidal wave of happiness and actualization," and the voice will say . . . *what if I told you that up those stairs, just a* little *farther, is a palace?*

I once stood eye-rolling in boiling Spanish July, surrounded by other fanny-packed Americans outside an ancient building. Apparently, it was a billion-year-old olive oil factory. But I was a spoiled teenager and had maxed out on listening for the day. We were a pack of shuffling, itchy tourists, dehydrated and sulking for the sandwiches the tour guide assured us were at the next stop. We were encouraged to visit the gift shop or pee, and then get back on the bus. It was six billion degrees and heritage-wise we were a group designed for boring poems in cold Anglican shade. Our dead eyes shared a quiet agreement that this would be a quick stop. But out of the doors burst the factory owner with different plans.

His English was not great but that didn't stop him. He was going to give us a fucking tour whether we liked it or not. And he was going to start with the history of the olive itself. And the folly of his great-grandfather, and the way the wind changes every bottle, and that Italy doesn't know fuck about soil, and please, *please,* I see talking in the back, *silencio,* the year was 1801, and Fernando el Primero had nada. *Nada.* Please, please. *Listen.*

It went on for so long. He lacked any sort of ease or charm in the tour, no feeling of pull up a sourdough and let me tell you a tale. Instead it was a crazed emergency, spit flying and hands landing a plane from Pluto. The need and import were at a twelve. When he motioned for the group to follow him to the back so we could begin Intro to Machinery, I waffled like the rest, desperate for Tetris on the bus.

But no. To my horror, I heard the *whipwhipwhip* I'd known my whole life as the sound of my father's khaki shorts whisking together in his signature walk, a breakneck stride that screams, *This infant is not going to fucking die on me, not today.* My mom and I exchanged *no God no* eyes. My brothers searched the dust for answers. My dad was hot on the man's heels, asking follow-up questions about the drought of 1932. Over his shoulder, he made graveyard eye contact with me, pointed a missile across the courtyard to my sternum, then pointed after the man. Wanting to continue life beyond that day, I obeyed my father.

Inside, the man continued to chide us for not listening and continued to not make much sense. A story was so boring that I replayed *101 Dalmatians* in my head to see if I could remember the plot. Roughly sixteen years later our tour guide clapped and lamented excuses for freedom. We Chads and Kathys formed a polo-ed line back onto the bus, muffling giggled misery and impressions. My dad hung back from the crowd in the ancient dust. He sighed to the sky.

"It's like doing a matinee." I started to laugh and stopped when his voice broke.

My dad was crying. After a helpless collection of seconds, I put my left Ked near his right New Balance. I hated that I was old enough to know what he meant.

It was like a matinee. Baring your soul to a group of people who don't want it. Or want the gift-shop version. Gripping people by the collar and saying, *Look, look, it's the light inside me, I* need *you to see it,* and the person saying, *I have to pee.*

Later I saw it for myself. There have been moments onstage where I thought I felt the little internal light come out my mouth and float in the room, where I thought, *This is it, it's happening.* And then you look up and see another light. Of a cell phone. Of someone so bored at your attempt at magic that they need to see if the Phillies scored.

I have been them, too, standing at a friend's girlfriend's art show agape at her paintings that to me looked like *Sesame Street* compost. Scrambling to fill silence I told her I found them "fun." Her resulting facial expression sent the message that she'd find it "fun" to pour me a turpentini. I later overheard her tell a turtle-neck that the piece was inspired by her "attack."

I counted myself a genius for knowing from the beginning that societal success had nothing to do with inner-light recognition. I would pursue the former; the latter, however, was for other people. Lucky, vain people. I would aim to support myself however I could as an actor. I would have *that* be the big dream, and have it be my mortifying secret that I thought there was something specific and special buried in there, desperate to come out. But oh well, it would just never have the chance to. I would swing for the fences in parts I was given, but there would never be *the one.* I patted myself on the back for knowing lotion sponsorships and statues didn't make you happy. I did convenient math. I blanket-associated self-worth with vanity, ambition with self-obsession. And that led me to . . . *hide.* Trying to unearth my own inner pinprick of light would be stupid. Embarrassing. Unrealistic.

What I of course meant is it would hurt too much. I'd rather cling to a safer story—that maybe I *could* have a moment of magnificence, but was simply never given the chance. Instead of the horror of being given the chance and being . . . mediocre. Or it happened and no one cared. I thought *that* would kill me. Once, while playing Monopoly with my brothers, I saw I was going to lose, so I yawned that I didn't want to play anymore. Deactivating heartbreak with a shrug at every turn. The light buried in me would die with me. By saying that outright, no one could hurt me.

There is one story in my family about a guy on the Irish side who there are no other stories about. All I know is he was a dark and complicated man made more dark and complicated by the war. He wrote obituaries at a local paper, a job he was insanely overqualified for. His brain may have been roiling with darkness, but it was brilliant. Apparently, the faraway *Time* magazine took notice of this—seeing a glimmer of strange light in an obituary in a paper eight hours away. They called him in for an interview.

The story goes like this. He put on a suit. He drove to the train. He took the train all day. He weaved through the city to the towering Time building. He walked into the lobby. He pressed the elevator button.

But the elevator took too long. So he turned around. And he came home.

More than death I am afraid of that. Of my ability to tilt the wheel toward the guardrail to beat the sheet of ice to it. I spent most of my life not hitting the elevator button to protect myself.

Then out of nowhere I stood screaming for it, naked and sobbing in the lobby, saying, "Hurry, hurry, I don't know when I'm going to turn around."

13

BRAINWOMEN

Maybe I think so much in metaphor because a metaphor almost killed me. Something happened when I was thirty, something so profoundly weird that it sounds like a lie. If someone told me this story, I would nod aloud *Whoa that's insane* and silently think *I am embarrassed for this liar.* This was the first thing I told every doctor when it was happening: I know this looks like a lie. I am on *your* side. This is insane, let's make fun of me. But also—am I going to die?

It happened at a moment where things were moving very fast. I wanted to text God asking if we could pause. After ten years of trying, I found that my career had begun to suddenly pick up. It was what I had always wanted, but I also wondered why it felt so fraudulent. Finally my resume and romantic life were both seizing in the way I had dreamed they might someday. I had a career and a partner. Why did it feel wrong? I started thinking about my brain, about why I was the way I was. How did I get here? And thus began the metaphor-thinking that my now therapist has requested we be selective with. (Last session she took off her glasses and asked, "Wait, stop. Am I the pine tree or are you?")

But this was the first time I stopped and tried to understand. This is when I came to the obvious and only conclusion. My brain is a room full of women who take turns at the wheel. It's the only way I can make sense of what it feels like to be alive. Mine stand in a conference room behind my eyes, looking out at my day and taking the controls when summoned. Some of them have been dormant for years, napping on crumpled blazers by the Keurig, waiting to be needed. But my key players are as follows:

Joni McLamb coos at babies and weeps when she realizes the old lost mumbling man on the C train isn't wearing a wedding ring. Crags Garafalo handles Time Warner Cable and street harassment. Blanche VonFuckery calmly gathers her blood-colored ballgown and crosses to the controls with her quivering goblet when my partner says things like "I mean, my passion is cooking, and yours is vacuuming, right?" Veronica Curvingham sees a sedated lumberjack in a Sbarro and attempts to ruin his life with the way she drops and picks up a straw. Ariel Gutknife journaled the shit out of 2003 and takes your brain on a what-if-maybe dreamthink during financial discussions. Ingrid St. Rash tries to convince you every zit is proof you're a lesion to society and puts incoming compliments directly in the Betty Company shredder. Later, Shirley Tinsel tapes them together, smiling through her braces at the words she can make out.

Here I land at the terrifying secret. I don't have the crucial one. I don't have a Sheryl Manila. I see her in the eyes of every one of my best friends—one hand on the hip of her perfectly tailored pantsuit, the other shading her chic smoky eye, searching in vain for the corresponding Sheryl in my brain. She's not there. But I love to watch her work for my friends. Sheryl boldly asks after the milkshakes we ordered fifteen minutes ago, and while she understands that this baby shower is not a contest, she WILL make the best flower crown possible so that she will win the . . . you know . . . contest. She demands that your insurance company explain why a mole removal cost more than your refrigerator.

Most importantly, Sheryl stays up nights and transcribes your other brainwomen's poems and prayers into concrete plans. She waves away Ingrid's insistence you don't deserve it and Joni's fear you will alienate people along the way. Sheryl is going to take you by the wrist and march you to your destiny—whether it's for your rightful place in the Starbucks line or your rightful salary. Even when your other brainwomen are at the wheel, Sheryl is there, backseat-driving for your future.

With no Sheryl of my own to do this, I carefully crafted my identity to never need her. I wanted a career, yes, but as an *actor*. This allowed me to cheat the system. For years, I tried to make a living out of letting the fearful, darker-souled brainwomen sing what they see. I didn't want a Sheryl there to tell them to be reasonable, or to take care of themselves: I was afraid they'd stop showing me their view of the world. I wanted to swim in the questioning, terrifying territory that my women led me to. In return, I promised them a life that wouldn't be too loud or extraordinary: I knew that with no Sheryl we couldn't handle that. In a character, I'd work my ass off and risk and try. My business emails around said job would be riddled with apologies and never minds. I worked, and socialized, but with long months of shades-drawn-couch-hiding in between to assure myself the beta life was the best fit for me.

Then I started to lead the wrong life. After ten years of an acting job or two a year, I was suddenly working without a break. One month exploded with logistics that were meant to fill a full year. I was playing a Voldemort drag Barbie on *Masters of Sex,* in Los Angeles. I was also trying to keep my East Coast relationship alive. I was also set to be a bridesmaid in Dani's wedding and at the icy-turned-sister actress wedding, one week apart in New York. Every Friday I got on a red-eye back East, to either hold a friend's bouquet or water my relationship. With filming and flying and not sleeping, there was *no* time. I had to become a logistics ninja. Me, the woman who once invited people for dinner and when they arrived realized I didn't have napkins or chairs. I went to Dani's wedding swaying and wired from a red-eye, checking my phone during the ceremony to make sure I wouldn't miss the return red-eye that night. To save time I inhaled a tequila instead of dinner and flew back to LA. I walked directly from LAX to the hair and makeup trailer to the set to my knees. To mime a cable-sanctioned blow job. It felt like the wedding had been a dream.

Then in the busiest week of my life, I got the biggest job I ever tried for. A type of thing that I had *not* gotten so many times that I had long given up on it happening. It was called *GLOW*—a show about female wrestling. Naturally. Definitely the biggest part I'd ever had on-screen. September was already foie gras–ed with shit to do and planes to be on, friends to be there for and hours to work. I now had to fit in hours of a calm, soothing activity: wrestling. As in, Hulk Hogan–style, slam your bones into a (NOT-PADDED SIDEWALK-FEELING) mat. Namaste.

I immediately began wrestling training between filming *Masters.* I'd get up at 3:30 a.m., work out, scream-drive through traffic to *Masters,* try not to be a terrible actor until rush hour, scream-drive through traffic to wrestling training, snort coffee before four hours of body slams, scream-drive home, and wake up to do it again. And again. And again. I tried to Frankenstein a Sheryl out of my brainwomen, but they were in hysterics, sobbing into their bathrobes, trying to teach themselves Excel and linear thinking. It's fine, I thought, it's *one month,* and it will calm down. Once I get through this three-jobs-overlap-month I will be fine. This is what all my successful actor friends had done for years while Crags and Ingrid had me YouTubing game show winners. I could fake a Sheryl. I had to.

I was terrified of getting injured while flipping and throwing humans on no sleep. So I did what I know how to do. I found an alpha woman to help me. I began daily "physical therapy" with my favorite LA fixture—an opinionated ex-actor-new-age-kook from Yelp. Every day, she ground her witch-at-KISS-concert acrylics into my muscles until I screamed. Wearing bedazzled aqua sweatpants, she used some *Star Wars*–looking machine to pump electricity through my upper body. I was trying to whip Joni and Ingrid and the rest into a corporation, forgetting that it was their tiptoeing with arms wide that got me here.

I was soon reminded.

Six days before *GLOW* started filming, it happened. I was lying on the therapy table of my crystal-toting, reality-show-pitching, unstable physical therapist. I'd had two hours of sleep, filmed all day, wrestled for four hours, returned my forest-green bridesmaid dress as per Dani's bark-text, and was doing the mental JetBlue red-eyes math to be back in time for the first day of *GLOW.* An opportunity I could not. Fuck. Up.

Then, slowly, it began.

It was so tiny at first that I thought I was imagining it.

My left shoulder started to jump. It was minuscule, like I was dancing the smallest mouse dance possible to a continuous beat. I laughed a little at it. Then the shrugging began. My shoulder leapt up to my ear, stayed there locked for a few seconds, then rolled back intensely, the muscles in my upper back seizing and flexing. Ingrid reminded me that the first priority was not to appear high maintenance, so I waved it off and naturally . . . got in my car.

To get on the highway.

There, in standstill 405 traffic, my entire upper body began to dance. From neighboring cars, it must have looked like I was the first person to ever rage-dance to the Grateful Dead. It was a continuous violent spasm that shot from my left hand, up my arm, across my shoulders, down the right arm, and back again. It sent me jerking forward and my body rolling backward, like Elaine Benes on a dance floor in Hades. I could not stop what was happening. It was terrifying. I was saying, "You're OK, it's OK, shh shh shh la la la" like a self-demon-doula, then Crags laughed for a while, and then it was very quiet. I tilted the mirror on myself. The spasms yanked me against the seat belt so hard I had a deep red line across my neck.

I somehow made it back to where I was staying alone without shake-driving into the ocean. I sat sobbing in the kitchen in the dark while my body shook and writhed—arms all the way up to the sky, then suddenly plummeting to the ground. Both shoulders tensed in a rock-hard shrug, frozen there for minutes at a time. Patrick came over with sushi and jokes; he was like my mother that way, could make you cry-laugh on the worst day of your life. But when he hugged me goodbye, I saw the flash on his face of real fear. I tried to breathe and assure the brainwomen that whatever this was would pass. But I couldn't hear them.

It lasted six days.

I went to the doctor the next morning, as it would have been vain to go immediately. I terrified the waiting room by sitting there sobbing while angrily noodle-dancing in my pajamas. I've been to enough Phish shows to know how insane I looked. Have you ever had a doctor walk in, see you, and scream, "HO"? I do not recommend. I was given some Mister Ed dose of a *Real Housewives* pill—after the doctor took a video to "show his students." I then casually Ubered to the set of *Masters of Sex* to um, film a scene. Calling in "sick" to work when you're an actor on TV means so many thousands of not-your-dollars lost and literally *hundreds* of people mad at you. You think Joni was going to let that happen?

The Uber driver assuredly thought I was on some form of tribal meth. My arms made a fence post and claw hands and shook while I tried a calming "HUUUUUUUUUUUUU" for the ride's duration. At *Masters,* I sat in the hair and makeup trailer and showed off some new fun spasms, like a violent flamenco shimmy that lasted twenty minutes. Tears poured down my face and no one spoke. Just the awkward clinking of curling irons for two hours. I remember a quiet and famous Silicon Valley actor coming in to get a haircut next to me, and no one explaining to him what was going on, not that anyone knew. His wide eyes stared lasers forward as I attempted a tight smile to say, *Hey, this is normal.* It felt like a *Curb Your Enthusiasm / Black Mirror* blend.

Filming the scene itself was its own pageant of horror hoops. We changed the blocking to hide the mutant dance—I was originally supposed to be standing. Now I sat behind a table cross-pinning my legs over my arm to keep it from shooting up into the air. But it did, many times. When I'd feel it about to happen,

I whispered, "Sorry, it's happening" to my scene partner, and my body would go into a Quasimodo jazzercise for a few minutes while the entire crew quietly coughed and shifted. I had been to Dani's wedding days before, and now I sobbed to my other friend on the phone that I couldn't make her wedding. The friend whom I'd fallen in love with in the background of the murder movie. When the terrible thing happened where you see text ellipses appear and then disappear, I sent her a video of me as a human maraca in the ER. She called me immediately, screaming. We also, of course, laughed.

I spent the weekend going to twelve doctors. No one knew what was happening; no one had seen it before. One ventured that my nervous system was having a panic attack, but had no idea what to do. "You just have to calm down and take a break." My dream job started in two days. One of the first scenes was a daylong wrestling match.

So, like any sensible actor with a disease that feels made up, I found a fucking witch.

Under the guise/lie of "massage," this woman was straight up Mad Madam Mim as a thirty-five-year-old with a dirty apartment. I walked in with my new physical norm, which was essentially doing the *Thriller* choreography on a galloping horse. She smiled and waved me in casually.

"My cat is here, but he never comes in the workroom, don't worry. He hates people."

The second I lay down on her table I heard paw-pattering and then felt a doughy thud on my chest. I opened my eyes to Pringles the cat looking at me with what I can only describe as Morgan Freeman realness.

"Oh my God . . ." the witch said under her breath. (If this is a gag she does with every client, I don't care. It was effective.)

"OK. Let's get started."

She gently shifted and touched me for a while, speaking softly while Pringles kneaded my sternum. For the first time in six days, I started to calm down.

"Can we do something weird?"

Mentally scrolling through my theatre school images of birthing a ball of light while my classmates held my hands, I assured her that for this here gremlin person, weird was impossible.

"Can you talk to her?"

". . . ."

"Whoever is scared."

Oy. But I already wrote the check and Pringles was waiting so here we go.

"K."

"Tell her you're OK."

Violent spasm.

". . . You're OK."

"What else?"

I sighed and dug deep into the former stoner recesses of my abstract dream bullshit capacity. I tried to walk around and look at Joni and Ariel and Ingrid and all of them. For the first time in months, I tried to listen to them. Who was screaming?

"How old is she?" the witch asked.

Hoo boy. Crags Garafalo was walking toward the brain mic ready to shut down the operation when this flew out of my mouth:

". . . Nine."

My arms shot into the air like a zombie playing the harp.

"What is nine for you?"

" . . . "

" . . . "

" . . . "

" . . . I guess . . . shame."

Spasms like a hypothermia victim balancing on an old-timey caboose.

"You're OK."

" . . . You're OK."

"What's she afraid of?"

Under my closed lids I rolled my eyes and stifled a laugh. And then big gnocchi-sized tears made a river to Pringles.

"That I'll forget her. That I'll leave her behind."

"Tell her you won't."

"I won't."

" . . . "

"I won't."

" . . . "

"I won't."

I lay there holding her hand for an hour, and without realizing when it happened, I was finally still.

I called my new bosses and told them we had to change the schedule, because I, um, had a weeklong, full-body muscle spasm that, like, stemmed from childhood stuff, and untended self-worth issues? I spent the days leading up to filming having conversations that would have sent pre-body-apocalypse Betty to the fear hospital. But my once-crowded brain now had a morning-after-Pompeii placidity, where apologizing for being alive now felt sort of . . . dumb. To my shock, no one screamed or died.

On the other end of the phone were the women I worked for. They got there by having conversations that scared them.

I took care of myself. I breathed in and I breathed out.

Slowly the brainwomen reappeared, ready. Now with a new one—a nine-year-old who we'll call Scraps. She has chocolate on her face and tangles that border on nests. And one more brain-woman appeared:

Fuckin' Sheryl.

14

THANKSGIVING

There's some fable that I won't google now as a point of pride (too many procrastination windows currently open in my Safari: disheartening porn, weatherman bloopers, and in a twist Skeet Ulrich Wikipedia dear god this book will never get written if I leave this page), but I know/think the fable is about two bugs. One spends the summer gathering berries and shit for winter hibernation, and one spends it dancing like a homeless fool doing ecstasy and having affairs. Or the fable-bug equivalent of that . . . so . . . let's say rhyming and square dancing. Then when winter comes, one bug has a mini-Costco bomb shelter of safety, and the other is mortgage-less, alone, and fucked. The latter had more fun, though. The fable always confused me. Which is maybe why I forgot 98 percent of the details. Which is a better life spent: berry hoarding or square dancing?

Anyway, at this point in life I was certainly the bug in the town square. Any time a dentist receptionist handed me a receipt or form and said the horror-words "for your records" . . . I shuddered. I pictured the haunted wicker basket under my bed where

I shoved government documents for three months before I panicked and threw them in the recycling. Or rather *on* the recycling, right on top in a neat pile for some Talented Mrs. Ripley
to come identity-xerox me if she wanted. In my Houston Street
apartment shared with Dani and other stoned, split-ended wise-
crackers, I did not put any tacks or nails in the wall or take vitamins. I was allergic to permanence.

In a Camel-smoke cloud of denial, I invited the one in Harlem
that I insisted wasn't my boyfriend home for Thanksgiving. As
was custom, we Gilpins braced ourselves for a WASP holiday, dry
piles of soft wartime rations on each inherited *Birds of America*
plate. Spice, flavor, and vulnerability of course prohibited by law.
Though we did pepper in our own elfish fun to deviate from the
silent fork clinking of our non-carnie ancestors. Inevitably my
mother would wrap her napkin on her head to do her screaming
Pope schtick, and my father would tell a moving story involving
a Whitman stanza and Yogi Berra adage. We do not know how to
season our food, but we do know how to entertain.

Having already raised the eyebrow of every friend and New
York bartender with the politics of our arrangement, my blue-
eyed plus-one and I knew a decision had to be made to say
goodbye or do something drastic, the relationship equivalent of
putting a tack in a wall. Which I of course hated, hated that I
couldn't tread water forever in the safety of not having to know
for sure if he loved me or not. Investment was too painful. *Maybe
this Thanksgiving is our funeral,* I thought.

While we were both pilgrim-looking people from New England, we couldn't have been raised more differently. He was
born on a barn floor into a circle of capable hallucinating lum-
berjacks and nurses wearing wolfskin. A family of hippies with

trades, people you want on your deserted island, both for the hugs and the skills. He knew every tree type by leaf and liked to cook obscure organs with peppers that made my eyes rain. He could talk for an hour straight about the make of a table leg or a hawk's itinerary. As for me, when a printer is out of ink, I fantasize about throwing the printer away. Thinking about how the wind works makes me crave a deep nap. He has talked about the wind to me for an hour. His name is, of course, Cosmo.

Still, here we were in a circle with my family, standing on the living room rug I once faux-skated backward across to emulate Tonya Harding. Tonya, whose team I was firmly on, spunky blonde in pink over whining Republican dentist in blue! (No evidence that Nancy Kerrigan was a Republican or a dentist, but brunettes with good teeth always make me feel this.) My father was enunciating through a pre-turkey prayer and asked us to close our eyes and think of something we had that we didn't deserve.

I peeked at my date's feet, which were at the moment somewhat upsetting. To the delight of my brothers, within the first fifteen minutes of our arrival, Cosmo had done something insane. In the midst of a loud-talking contest with my father (their one Venn diagram overlap) about wiper fluid, my father gestured an apology to my date's bare hobbit feet having to spend the holiday naked and cold in our no-shoes home. Realizing that all of us had aging Christmas Walmart "house socks," a look formed in his blue eyes that I could later identify as Must Do Immediate Elaborate Inconvenient Project to Fix Social Situation. Wildly air-traffic-signaling my father to continue his anecdote about 1983 John Lithgow, Cosmo disappeared under the kitchen sink. He emerged with an armful of paper grocery bags and blue duct tape. Energetically nodding and interjecting the occasional

"WOW," he got on all fours on the kitchen floor. Suddenly he was HGTV Hulk, violently ripping the bags like he was gutting a deer on a timer, making sure to return intense "I'm listening, totally here with you" eye contact with my monologuing father. Who seemed miraculously unphased by my date's inexplicable craft tornado. My brothers and I shifted in expired Old Navy around him, pretending the paper ripping wasn't too insane a volume to continue a discussion over. *What a wild end,* I thought. *Is he making a nest to take a shit on before breaking up with me in front of my family?* But then the tornado got smaller and quieter. He was cradling and shaping something, softer movements close to his chest, a gentle silent sculpt. As my father rounded the corner to the anecdote's punchline that my brothers and I could mouth word for word (DAD I LOVE YOU NEVER STOP THESE STORIES), this wild tinkering Tarzan sat back on his heels to reveal his creation. "What the *fuck,*" one of my brothers exhaled.

There in the center of chaos sat . . . beautiful, somewhat perfect . . . *trash slippers.* Shoes. Functional shoes. Made of trash. Confirming my suspicion that there would be no "tada" or explanation, he fired two passionate follow-up questions to my dad while sliding his feet into his creations, now a strange homeless *Sesame Street* medieval cobbler that I had brought into the home. It was my father who forced the acknowledgment, holding his hand up for silence in what I feared was disgust. But no, it was my father's specific holy reverence reserved for walk-off home runs and good sentence structure. (The highest honors.) He clapped the untamed cobbler on the back with admiration. "*This!* Is a *man!* A man with *solutions!*"

Post-slippergate, my solution-man dutifully circled the property with my mom. Linking her arm in his, she detailed the history of her contraband ivy collection, snippings literally stolen from Versailles and Harvard and replanted here, their backstories spoken at a louder volume than the hushed-but-sadly-still-audible jabs at her daughter "THESE ARE THE AZAELEAS well she's *always* been like that—you know when she first got her *license*? I mean, my *God*, YES THESE *ARE* PERENNIAL."

I worried that having him here would feel like reading the results of your colonoscopy at a burlesque show. A mood-killing spell-breaking fluorescent *you-can't-fire-me-I-quit*.

But my dad said, "Close your eyes and think of something you have that you don't deserve," and I peeked across the circle to those insane paper shoes and scanned up to his knees, muddy from an investigation into my mother's unruly daylilies, up to his mechanic-with-military-history torso that at night ran at a thousand degrees against my back even when I insisted falsely that I hated to be held, up finally to those stupid blue eyes that like a rubber band *duh* were already open looking back at me.

15

TRYING

A few years in we gave up the charade and found an apartment together. Much to the chagrin of one or two of my lingering condescenders (they didn't care) and a few of his I'm-a-little-teapot underwear-less hostesses (they cared). One such heartbroken schnauzer sent a postcard to the apartment early on, drunk on vacation with her girlfriends. I helpfully sat down with the kitchen scissors and cut the heart-dotted note into strips until it was a cup of dust, at which point I presented it to my now official boyfriend. "Mail for you!" Sadly no such scorned pageantry could be applied to the one or two measly "You still in town?" 3:00 a.m. texts I got from actor x and bored author y, the brand of men banished to sleep in their home office because they keep texting handfuls of former female protégés and not asking their wives questions. Eventually our respective HPV phone trees got the message that against all odds, we both had unsubscribed. He had picked me, and I had picked him. The loud sneezer. The cowboy with the aloe plant. Cosmo.

The apartment was on the top floor of a Harlem brown-stone—apparently historically where the maids' quarters of the house would be, as in summers it got so hot and stifling no spoiled madam in a corset would have survived. Our aging landlady lived on the first floor like a judgmental gatekeeper, tsk-ing behind her door at late-hour drunk entries and plugging her ears in shock when I told her we weren't married. "And we never will be," I couldn't resist adding when I sensed a Republican tint to the conversation. The stairwell featured colored-pencil sketches of different towns in Alaska, which made me hopeful and sad that she had some heartbreaking *what-could-have-been* fur-wrapped affair there but was now doomed to the solitude of peering through scalloped curtains at me sneaking cigarettes. I had told him I'd try to quit, a huge sacrifice, my favorite thing, my touchstone to you-don't-*really*-have-me. As usual, I was just outsourcing depth to something that only made me wheeze and smell bad.

We were very in love, but we were still playing chicken. So little things that seemed unrelated were actually behind-the-back gestures of permanence we were too scared to say out loud. Scrolling petfinder.com was one such brazen subliminal act of . . . *I'd like to keep being with you longer than a cough drop.* Without having to look at each other and say it.

This is all to say there wasn't a ton of logical reasoning for it, but we somehow decided to get a dog.

We first found Jay, a cinnamon mastiff whose profile stated proudly that he had severe PTSD activated by bicycles, certain hats, and joyful children. His bio said it was best to drape a thick blanket over your arm on walks with which to rapidly engulf Jay, in case you should encounter one of these triggers. Jay's delivery fell through at the last second, hopefully because he had found a home in the country where he wouldn't have to be shrouded so frequently. Thinking now that what came next was an accident or backup choice turns my stomach, makes me so sorry for the quantum me that's living a life out there without ever knowing Babe.

If I were his canine wingman and his Petfinder page was his dating profile, I would have offered some gentle notes. The pictures did not do his majesty justice. In fact, as advertised he looked a little like a Fraggle lizard or a nervous pig. Babe was a scrawny spaniel-and-pit-bull mix, a copulation that I don't think involved roses or consent. He was only one-ish, but his facial expression said, *Move on* and *I've seen wars*. Which of course his profile assured us he had. (Life is too sad to list the horrors here, but suffice it to say that people were evil to him. Evil.) But I reminded my creature-loving beau of the plan; this was a trial situation. We would *foster* him for a *month*. *Maximum*. We needed to be mature about whether or not a traumatized small lion would be a wise addition to our new home. No sudden moves.

At the end of day two of Babe's stay, I scream-sobbed across his fur that if anyone ever took him from me, I'd walk off a roof.

After a good bath and the subsiding of the bug-eyed terror, we realized this dog was . . . a regal beast of mythic descent. Seeing Cosmo and Babe side by side, I realized at once the eerie truth: they were . . . twins. Their wide-set eyes squinted in tandem a thousand yards ahead from their big block-heads with high cheekbones; both looked like a stoned Chinese New Year dragon with Kurt Russell feathering. I spent one glorious half day being Babe's favorite, solely from availability logistics and treat-baiting. I was swiftly replaced when the pup recognized the man he was dealing with. His human mirror. There is no greater love story than Babe and Cosmo.

I often hope that heaven is a sort of TED Talk convention forum, where you can dip in and out of angel-led retrospective PowerPoints on your own life and time as a whole. *You Were Once in the Same Footlocker as Your Future Husband in 1994 and Didn't Know It,* or *Soulmates That Missed Each Other by Forty or Three Hundred Years,* or *The Best of the Best: Superior One-Night Stands and Pies Throughout Time.* If there was one such seminar on animal-human connections throughout all of history, Cosmo and Babe would get at least an honorary slide.

Incorrect in my assumption I would be the doting mother of the pack, I was instead immediately demoted to a sort of embarrassing little sister. Babe all but rolled his eyes at me when I entered a room and writhed in mortification when I force-pulled him against me to snuggle. But Cosmo was his Jedi hunter tracker ESP sensei, a silent language between them with strict rules and binoculars to the world. Cosmo had to tell Babe something only once and it was rule forever. One stern "no" and a point at the carpeted bedroom meant Babe did not touch his paw on that carpet one single time, ever again. Instead he would rest his chin on the wood floor a millimeter from the door frame like a copper-eyed sentry, counting sighs until Cosmo woke up. Babe flickered at Cosmo's side at the bank, the subway, the doctor, all places with signs and rules against canines, but somehow their brothers-across-species stakes made misty the eyes of even the most aloof waiters. Babe snarfed at our feet in wineries, at DMVs, and on red-eye flights, all from people seeing something unique and looking the other way.

I was not without purpose to the sentient beast living in my home. He idolized Cosmo and treated every day as an opportunity to prove his James Dean cool and Horatio loyalty to him. But of course, there are moments where the body has other plans. Over the years, I woke with a start in the middle of the night to two saucer eyes searing caffeine into my dreams, jolting awake to his panting face that said everything that he couldn't to Cosmo. *I have diarrhea.* Or *This thunder is scary, and you need to sit with me.* Or *There's a mouse, and I'm too gentle to kill it, but I don't want Cosmo to know.* And then an hour later, *I killed the mouse, and I'll never forgive myself, and you need to sit with me.* I would go to his "bed," a ridiculous Macy's purple chaise longue purchased for my mom's children's production of *Twelfth Night,* and sit with him there until his fear subsided, or walk him through littered, asleep New York while a liquid version of whatever venison limb Cosmo had gifted him earlier evacuated onto the freezing sidewalk. Every time it was unspoken: *Tell him and I'll never reluctantly half snuggle you once every two weeks again.*

Babe would sleep in positions that looked like he was a zero-gravity-koala on Valium, so serene and suspended in dangled-paw joy. After the first few days of anxious chewing and shaking at sirens, he shifted into a trust of the world and of us when neither had earned it yet. The first time he sunk the full weight of his chin onto my chest, eyes closed in sayonara sleep, I froze. I thought of how many times in my life I'd fallen asleep clenching or sighing or wincing, replaying that day's regrets and panicking about tomorrow's ifs. I wondered into his fur. If love is stillness and actualization is a fight, I didn't know how to get one without killing the other. I did want *this,* though. This snoring, trusting, feathery, and hopeful peace.

The three of us formed a strange band of sleepy, furrowed-brow cowboys. We were a family of course, the canine addition the missing link to our admitting this was it. It was unnerving. In my adulthood, "home" had always been whatever cereal-dusted storage unit I used to quick-change into the next ho-frock, or to sit out an ill-timed mushroom trip, or to futon-journal wintry depression musings until noodles arrived. All, of course, beautifully alone, immune to accountability, invisible to the world.

For this here crotchety jester, this recluse time was necessary. To play my various sidekick roles, I needed the drawbridge-retracted, me-island time. Even as a kid I kept my room sealed off as the place no one could go—locked in my annexed holy shrine for sad and mime. My brothers spilled their belongings and story lines out into the kitchen and dinner conversation; we knew about every bong and rash and crush. I, conversely, was a privacy samurai. Not understanding my darkness or how to control it myself meant I knew one thing for sure: it was no one else's to know about. Being alone in a literal locked room for hours was my necessary personality dialysis. Will only tap-dance if granted hermit time.

Yet another reason building a relationship was inconvenient. Cosmo joked that I liked knowing that a getaway car was ready for me at any point, idling in the driveway with Doritos and a new passport. Instead of assuring him, "Hush darling, that feeling is behind me," I said, "Oh for sure yah."

But like I said, these were cowboys. They had their sleepy warrior eyes on the horizon, too. No one in the club was asking picket fence questions. When I expressed interest in zigzagging the country for a decade of rootlessness to pursue this career of instability, my vagabond duo of wizened dudes was happy to oblige.

So we did. Every year the three of us drove cross-country from New York to LA for pilot season, this the era before apps and tampon brands made television year-round. Pilot season was a late-winter desperation pageant in Los Angeles. Think of it as a marathon in kitten heels, and the prize you get is to hold a folder near Heather Graham for your pension. It is the *Lip Gloss Hunger Games* of network television, a city of hungry memorizers fumbling through bronzer guesswork in traffic, begging, sobbing for coveted 911 Operator with a Past.

As horrific and heaving-snot-sob-heavy of a time pilot season was, it was the only window of opportunity I saw to get to a level where Cosmo could stop paying for every ramen. There were casting offices in New York of course. But for jobs that "moved the needle," making a tape in New York often felt like you were better off whispering your audition in Latin to a Times Square Elmo. Cosmo was able to do his sales job remotely, often speakerphoning staff meetings while shirtlessly bear-proofing our roadside campsite, his four-legged Tonto yawning at his side. I wonder how many dojo and salon owners noticed their scheduling-software demos had occasional road rage interjections.

We stopped at every national park we passed, when I was either hopeful and anxious en route to this year's California Try or dejected and bitter slinking home to this year's New York Oh Well. We drove different routes every time, if only to fool the matrix into thinking this year would yield a different result. We set up a one-person tent on the edge of glaciers and Arby's and bayous in the name of trying to raise my IMDb score. In Los Angeles we'd stay with my godmother above her garage in Brentwood, my mother urging me on the phone to time OJ's Bronco drive for myself.

The months in LA were my first taste of a dull hum of disconnect from self that the entertainment business can have on you. I always disliked Los Angeles, a fact that we New Yorkers love to offer up as an original trait like when drunk white girls say they love Halloween. But the feeling was authentic: I never understood the place. "Hikes" there are treeless mountains of dirt that lead to the center of the sun, surrounded by other people who are talking about the same script that you are, but with the absence of self-deprecation. "Meetings" are lattes in spaces that feel like Customs by Pinterest, while the shark you've been assured begged for the meeting says, "Right right right" before you get to the predicate of your sentence while their eyes flick to an entering Jonas. Wanting a stick of gum or envelope means entering a world of Black Friday car culture where not slamming on the gas the second a light turns green is grounds to be chased by a browned wax turkey in a Lexus who screams, "FUCK YOU FUCK YOU FUCK YOU" as they pass. The amount of time people will talk about their diet or exercise is limitless; Disorders can wear Health as invisibility cloaks and forge themselves as personalities. Strangely, as the Ultimate Goal has become to be hot for each other, so plummets actual sexiness. Sex is gross and dirty. Good sex requires a rabid fascination with the other person's body. Selfies are sterile and deceptive. They require a rabid fascination with your *own* body. I picture the waste that must be the adonni of LA having sex with each other, grossed out by each other's fluids, staring down at their own abs.

As a well-fed, grounded scientist, I find this sad.

I know now that this is just one sliver of that city. Where New York is a pulsing available puppy offering you everything all at once the second you open your door, Los Angeles is a series of secret pockets you have to seek out, a cat who's not going to give it up for free. Most of the best people I know live there, and the city has given me so much. But it is also all the things I mentioned, and seeking approval from a sad shell that doesn't want you . . . slowly turns *you* into a sad shell, too.

One year, for one particular pilot, I made it all the way to the network test. It was for the role of the crazy lesbian neighbor to the gorgeous lead. (I had originally auditioned for the lead; the speed with which the casting director suggested I trade audition sides in the hallway for Mrs. Macaroni next door was not *not* offensive.) A network test means you dress like you're going to your ex's wedding and say terrible memorized lines to a room full of silent senator-y dudes inexplicably in cashmere scrubs and a few humorless women who truly hate you. I had been on one trillion auditions, but this was my first network test—and apparently there were new rules. We were warned before we went in: *though this is a comedy, they will not, as a rule, laugh.* This confused me, as I thought laughing was an involuntary wonderful part of life but now understood it to be a last-resort option for approval, like a phallic bachelorette sticker for a child's bed-wetting calendar.

I entered the silent, sad, crowded room. I decided to give Mrs. Macaroni the character trait of her eyes crossing every time she sneezed, staying like that until she sneezed again. This joke landed like a milk-soaked dead seal. I was ready to launch my backup joke of giving her an uncontrollable kick when she walked, because of course this room was begging for a big swing risk. On the first kick I added a "HAH!" for good measure, and felt a shift near my calf.

I looked down and saw an illustration of my heart breaking.

A pair of my period-stained underwear that had apparently hitched a ride in the calf of my already pitiful jeggings was crowning at my sad elastic ankle hem. In the sole moment of togetherness, the room held its breath as I midwifed the underwear from the leg of my anticirculation pants. Reader, it was sad. I tried to play it off as a calculated reveal by answering the underwear like a phone and improvising a telemarketing call. I made the horrific mistake of looking up and making sweeping eye contact with the first row of apparently hundreds of executives in the room, all looking down, *Sophie's Choice* extras staring into the ground in mortification. I understood. It was the only time I understood them.

I was mercifully shown out to the lobby, where the four other auditioners were waiting, swimming in their own respective shame flashbacks. A shivering cardiganed intern appeared out of nowhere and vaguely asked us to leave. The five of us shuffled into the elevator in silence. Suddenly *four* of our phones rang. I answered mine, to a vanilla suicidal voice that exhaled ". . . stay in the elevator." When the doors opened, the one poor perfect woman whose phone didn't ring walked out. Suddenly realizing she was alone, she stopped, turning slowly to look back at the frozen four of us, perplexed why we weren't getting off. I will never forget the elevator doors closing on her saying the words "w-what are you guys—" and then the sound of the echoey lobby air sucked out by the squish of the doors, then our ears popping in dead silence. We quietly put our phones back in our bags, sad and dumb. (What became of you, fifth woman? I want for you a farm and billions.)

The four of us reauditioned for another two hours. None of us got the part.

It was not *all* horrible of course. When I did work, I loved it *so* much, even in the stuff that was clearly terrible or would never see the light of day. Everything was an education. I mostly cried and died on all the TV shows that insomniacs and procrastinators

watch on a loop, yelling out the murderer at the opening se-
quence of a seen-it-before episode. These jobs were a crash course
in dealing with people I would encounter for the rest of my career: Disgruntled Self-Proclaimed Genius Mad He Isn't Downey,
Out of Touch Melting Candleface Dame Mad You Exist, Director Afraid of Star So He Yells at You, and many, many more. But
mostly there were wonderful people, the best kind there are, the
most delicious fun smart infuriatingly brilliant people whom I
can't believe I got to be near, who saw me flailing and guessing and discreetly stepped in to steer me away from destruction.
All of these broken innocence-assassins and brilliance-diviners
made up a real-world school of how to and how not to be. The
ones who screamed for quiet and shunned homework were usually bad. The ones who knew names and lines and touched your
shoulder good morning were usually good. Embarrassing myself
on the sidelines, I also kept my eyes open to what the varsity team
was doing right and wrong. I quietly dreamed of the actor I might
like to be someday.

Thankfully Cosmo had seen me in the things that I was proud-
est of that otherwise only two random New York grandmothers
had seen. *He* knew that my dream had more to do with chasing
the memory of sitting diapered in the wings of the Cape Play-
house, squealing at the spotlight, inching illegally toward the lit
square where all the joy was happening. The dream had less to do
with actual success. He knew even when I forgot. He saw that
when I came home sobbing about not getting an arc on *CSI Tulsa,*
that it was because my brain was confused. That I was listening to
the wrong voices. That it was time to Etch a Sketch a reset.

Which being in love does, of course, over and over again. On one of our Uncle Sam pilgrimages, we stopped at Glacier National Park. It was after a particularly gutting pilot season, one where I had tested for a few things that would have entirely multiplied my tax return in a way that was almost funny. But alas they had gone to a nineties pop star and Australian print model, and one part had been written out of the piece entirely. I was up my own ass of sulking in my failure. The dull hum of world rejection and solipsism *that it all mattered so much* filled our car like a war-crimes-level dog fart. Which was of course also actually happening; Babe helpfully funneled a sense of tone from the back seat.

But in Glacier, my phone mercifully lacked reception. This made my cutting ritual of refreshing rejection emails and googling the winner impossible. We set up our tent near some skeptical goats and took a walk along the water. I kicked rocks in silence, letting the surrounding flora know I was in mourning for my pride. Could the tone-deaf eagles even *comprehend* how important one's career was?

Then one of those moments happened where you think, *Freeze this, remember this.* A splash snapped me out of my internal pity montage. Cosmo had jumped in the frigid glacier water, coughing through the feeling of his asthmatic lungs receiving an immediate ice-mammogram. He then ran around on the rocks naked and hooting, steam coming off him like he was on fire. All to make the sulktress laugh. Babe leapt around him in celebration, understanding that he had done something heroic. (Which was not as impressive, as he reacted the same when Cosmo sneezed or closed a car door.) I watched the strange tribal dance in a limbo pause, everything a little blurry for a second. Cosmo looked up at me. Eye contact for a few exhales. Then he pointed. A pointless point, just . . . at my face.

I inhaled sharply like a punch, three feet deeper into my body than I'd breathed in days. I suddenly felt like the park itself, a huge fissure in my chest open to the core of the earth. It was one of those feelings so big, you realize how small all the others have been. Much bigger than any brief hit of *yes* or sad hum of *no.* This man and that dog and this second of time, exploding me into the sky, shaking a sob out over the lake.

I shook my head across the shore at him. I waved helplessly through the surge. I was an idiot. Running around the world trying to feel loved does not compare one grain to loving someone else. Finding flickers of a twin in someone's eyes and hushed union in the dark of a theatre were beautiful, yes. Fleeting moments of sameness and recognition had felt like the thing to spend my life running toward. But there was something so much more thundering and beautiful here. Love that had nothing to do with stopping to make sure you exist. Instead of *Am I here? Do you see me?* You think, *Oh God. Look at you!*

Sensing the romance, Babe dramatically threw up some grass. I woke up that night in the tent with Babe's paw on top of our held hands, like we were a strange asleep contra-species Little League team.

In the dark I thought, *Chase your dream, Gilpin, sure. But don't let it ruin this. Don't drift off so far that you forget this, and suddenly it's too late to save it.*

I began to understand that the version of my life I thought I could seek out and control was not going to happen. That damming up progress on *this* side insisting it had to wait until progress on the *other* happened was not logical. There was not going to be a magic catapult that ensured commitment and breastfeeding wouldn't kill me. The right email was not going to reroute a future midlife crisis. Life was just going to happen. Flashbulbs and glacier lakes are two different highs. One a Pixy Stix that dies immediately, and one that alters your DNA and makes you sob in CVS a decade later remembering it.

There was a year I went to LA by myself. I can't remember why. But I spent a random month there trying to get a job. Maybe I even got one, an episode of something. But it was mostly the same Trying in Traffic routine. Cosmo and Babe were spared this particular trip for some reason. I FaceTimed them regularly. Even though this was my supposed holy *hermit just-me noodles-and-YouTube* retreat time, it felt wrong. I had grown accustomed to various canine and bro limbs and sighs, both elbowing me awake and the only way I could sleep. I missed those grunting snuggled charlatans. Cosmo answered one FaceTime from a familiar ratty quilt, the one in my childhood bedroom. I laughed to myself that the same person I spat whiskey at in a motel in a velour doll costume was the same guy checking my parents' gutters and making them goat stew they pretended to want.

I flew home after my last audition, realizing later that it was somewhat of a coup that my hair happened to be curled that day. Cosmo and Babe met me unexpectedly at the airport. Normally the embodiment of casual ebullience, they were distracted and formal. We drove home in uncommon silence.

. . . Huh.

I plopped down my luggage of Please Like Me uniforms that had failed to deliver and dove onto the purple chaise for some needed Babe forced-spooning. But Cosmo waved me solemnly into the bedroom.

OK, what the fuck is happening, I thought. Either he fucked someone or killed a postal worker or is now a Republican. I walked the plank to the bedroom.

Our once-naked box spring now backed up to a huge wooden headboard. It was three beams of shining, jagged wood, something that a harpooned mermaid might float to shore on. It was weird and beautiful and exactly us.

"It's from the apple tree at your house." I remembered suddenly that he had chopped down a tree in my parents' woods years ago, provoking a neck-craning eye roll from me when he insisted it was for a pending project. The wood then napped dormant in my parents' garage for years. Until, apparently, now, when he made secret trips there while I was away, milling and sawing and thinking about this moment.

I stared at the headboard.

He pulled out a box.

I stared at the box.

He asked me to marry him.

I felt like I was going to vomit.

Not butterflies vomit. More like *oh no oh no oh no* vomit. The explicit deal was that we were never going to do this. A literal, actual, spoken-aloud, and agreed-on *deal.* We had been together ten years now and everything was fine, wasn't it? And we always said that if anything, *I'd* propose to *him* if we felt the urge, which we promised we never would? *What the fuck is happening?*

I blinked through my vomit suppression at the box that . . . wait—had . . . *two* rings.

"There's a part of you that will always be just yours, that I will never know or understand. So. This is the 'no' ring. You can just . . . be married to yourself, and we can pretend this never happened."

(The walls were turning to LSD Jell-O.)

"But. There's also this one. For 'yes.' And I think we should do it. I want. I want you to marry me."

My brain was off-line.

". . . I . . . I was supposed to propose to *you*!"

He looked at me under the raised eyebrow like he does when I have chocolate on my face.

". . . You know that was never going to happen, B."

Oh fuck.

Uh. Yeah. Wow. I was probably never going to do that.

Because for all the progress I'd made, I was still nervously shuffling in the lobby of my life, too terrified to make a move.

Aware it was now my line, I cried and said yes. Yes, yes of course. But I still felt like I was stoned and there was a dead body on the floor, that there was something so intense and surreal happening and I was dazed and thinking about snacks. What was wrong with me?

I got out of bed at 4:00 a.m. and took Babe for a walk. I dreaded the internal crazy-summit I had to conduct. But it had to happen.

I took a deep breath and climbed the mental stairs to the women in my brain. I had to tell them the bad news. I'd given in and given up. They were not going to be fucking happy. They were all wildly different, all with opposing ideas of what my life should be. But I thought none—*none* of them—wanted to get *married*. I pictured their faces dropping in horror, screeching that this derailed their blueprints for whatever life of bold majesty or cowering bathrobe they prayed for, both paths contingent on solitude.

I walked through the dark and repeated aloud what Cosmo had asked me.

The brainwomen screamed. Their unified immediate reaction felt like a slap, and Babe raised his borderline human eyebrow when I stopped rigid on the pavement like I'd walked into a pole. I was shocked. Then suddenly I was caffeinated and sobbing and running, Babe's collar tinkling like Rudolph's bells sprinting next to me, elated to be pointed back toward the man that of course, of *course,* you fucking idiot, was the person you wanted to be near for the rest of your dumb life. Whom you apparently wanted, more than anything, to marry. The person every favorite and cursed part of you screamed for in unison *yes, yes, yes.*

16

FIXER-UPPER

After the reality set in that only Versailles mafia oligarchs could afford Brooklyn real estate, Cosmo and I began to browse north for our dream weekend-escape cabin. Since we were both New Englanders, we dreamed of peppering some pine trees and cider donuts back into our lives somehow. Maybe we could find something we could afford, a place to scurry to between sequels and soliloquies and waiting for the phone to ring. My bank account consisted of four hugs and a cough drop. Still, we scoured Zillow together. Our Brooklyn pantry stuffed with his thousand-tool museum, Cosmo assured me he could turn any haunted tornado shack into a Nancy Meyers–worthy celebrity rehab center while I valiantly napped. Or at least that's how my brain filtered the words "We would do the work ourselves."

We spent a year of weekends stepping through houses that had been on the market for years, their pictures conveniently omitting the beached uranium barge on the lawn. Every house closed my throat tighter. Slowly my *Gwyneth of Green Gables* fantasy turned into *Deliverance*. Cosmo was the happiest I've seen him. I stood in one kitchen marveling at a sink full of dusty ghost shoes when from deep in the woods he shouted, "This is where we'd build the compostable toilet!"

Later that year, through sobs, I had to tell him that a shack only accessible by boat would kill me. No coffee or girlfriends for miles and the sound of branches scratching on shingles were a recipe for me to slip off the raft. But buy a house we did: a faded red 1834 farmhouse that said Abigail Adams on the outside and *Duck Dynasty* on the inside. It was filled with what a sunnier, more-caffeinated person might call "cool challenges." Tiny stairs designed for miniature colonial feet. Aggressively stained wallpaper, some of it decorating what I lovingly referred to as the "Guantánamo Room." Brown wall-to-wall carpeting everywhere—including the kitchen. A gaping hole in the ceiling that surely housed thousands of mouse cadavers, and possibly a transparent eyeless blacksmith.

Cosmo spent our first day as homeowners taking stock of the needed repairs. I had never seen such a burly man *skip*. I sat on the porch and stared at what I was sure was my new best friend: the middle distance. The next day Cosmo took me on a tour of the thousands of fix-it projects he was raring to complete. He was so adorably excited that I knew telling him my throat was closing would be cruel. But at the next reveal I could not keep the drama at bay. He unveiled the grand finale: hiding in an old chicken coop was a new drum kit.

"I'm going to learn the drums!" he proclaimed.

I slid onto the grass and screamed. I suddenly knew what was waiting for me here.

Have you ever seen a woman realize that she has toothpaste on her shirt, nervously laugh for your benefit, then slowly look like she's going to murder six people? Believe her and step away.

There is a very convincing threat for some women that if we don't find the right job or serum or therapist or life secret, if we don't solidify our confidence in time, the demon that splattered the toothpaste will take over and rule for eternity. When she's in charge, she stashes important mail in a shoebox for six months, lets your hair tangle into a sad nest, puts the kettle on, and promptly leaves the house. The demon appears periodically to remind you that she's waiting for her grand takeover, laughing at your adorable attempt to organize the closet. I spent my life running terrified from her—cycling through selves like I was a paper doll, sure that the *next* version of me would be the antidote. I felt the demon snapping at my ankles as I ran, believing the world when it told me that men had the answer and girls had to guess.

At first the house only confirmed this belief. Cosmo skipped around the property with tools that looked like Tower of London souvenirs, gleefully ripping out drywall. He was flourishing. I was drowning. So much of my life as a woman had been dedicated to running, calculating, morphing on command. I didn't know how to do anything permanent. And here was a house whose roots went to the core of the earth. Little by little, it showed itself to me.

When we ripped up the carpet in the kitchen and then the wood underneath that, we found oak floors with burn marks where the oven had once been. Under one layer of floral wallpaper was another, a hand-painted scene of a woman walking down an Italian street. Brushing my teeth one night, I noticed a small slit inside the ancient medicine cabinet. A swift googling told me that's where old-timey people would dispose of razor blades, and that the entire wall was probably full of them. We pulled a bright green back seat out of the attic and put it on the front porch. Months later a six-thousand-year-old neighbor told us she'd ridden in the car it belonged to as a girl. The next time we came up from Brooklyn, she'd left iris bulbs at our door.

Gardening. That's something I could do, I realized. I'd had a summer job as a gardener when I was eighteen. Margot and I would show up stoned with rakes, joining a pack of teenage girls deadheading pansies in string bikinis, desperately hoping the bro-mowers would tell us where that night's kegger was. A frantic race to be accepted as the person we were not. Before the demon could get us.

At the farmhouse, the spade I found in the garage broke by the fourth bulb, so I just used my hands for the rest. In an hour I was covered in dirt and mud. But I was surprised at how much I remembered, how natural it was. I had assumed my eighteen-year-old self was too busy being an apologizing chameleon to retain anything as eternal as the subtleties of soil.

Maybe I was wrong in assuming my life had been an imper-manent scramble for identity. Maybe if I turned around and faced the toothpaste demon, I'd see she had never wanted to kill me. Instead she'd been watching me, picking up the things I'd thrown aside as useless or terrifying and secretly braiding them into an identity more powerful and ancient and beautiful than any pa-per doll. Maybe the greatest trick of all is to convince girls that their roots are weeds, that their powers are curses. Maybe we're taught to run and change because if we stopped and stood, the world would change.

People driving by saw a laughing mud woman on her lawn, hundreds of years old and full of razor blades.

17

THE GLIMPSE

To my disbelief, I saw it. For a tiny second, as in a second on an ant's wristwatch, they let me in.

I saw the Palace.

The fabled *Brigadoon* of the fancy level of actor, where it wasn't invisibility next to a waiting room orchid anymore but borrowed silks next to a tray of rock shrimp. It was a true shock that my career took this shiny turn. Usually for women, you're granted Palace entry when your skin is still placental, and only once within the Palace gates are you sometimes allowed to eventually turn thirty. But somehow, after over a decade of traffic sobbing and monologuing into the void, the coat check girl at the Palace was like . . . *you know what, fuck it, you can come it for a* second.

Let's be clear: I was and am still not an actual shiny person, or famous, or a millionaire. In terms of the Palace, I was *barely* legally permitted on the grounds. If Scarlett Johansson is Marie Antoinette and Brad Pitt is Louis XIV, I am a dysenteried, eyeless groundskeeper allowed *some*times to change bedpans if I have enough bread and loose teeth to trade for midnight entry.

But I've seen it, you know. The inside. It's wild.

GLOW gave me many things. Most astonishingly it gave me the chance to exercise Salem muscles while encased in Barbie garb, all on camera, for a living. And some people watched. It's certainly not like the old days where being on a TV show meant your life metamorphosed, and you were stopped in the street, and offers and praise diarrhea-ed into your lap. Now there are six thousand shows instead of twenty, and aside from being less panicked about rent, you find your life doesn't really change all that much. But *GLOW* got a little attention for a second, and I found myself in a strange position of sitting across from people whom I had begged for jobs for a decade who now said things to me like "Where have you been *hiding*?!" Um . . . In my rental Nissan sobbing in your casting parking lot, Gina. But sure, I'll play along. "I don't know . . . around!"

The little wave of "buzz" (kill me and kill this word) that the show got opened tiny doors for me to the hallway to the vestibule to the moat to the border guard to Ellis Island to the three riddles troll bridge guy to the Palace. For the first time, I saw a path to a life much more glittery than anything I'd dreamed of belting *South Pacific* into a Proactiv bottle.

But.

Palace entry is not a linear system based on merit and circumstance. Palace entry is bought. You have to first enter the zeitgeist somehow, sure, and maybe that's from being good in something and working very hard, and listen, if so that's beautiful and you should cheers yourself in a vintage mirror. But I learned quickly that there is no Show Biz Santa. A lot of the magic around someone having a "moment" is paid for, and white-knuckled, and a full, booming, churning business unto itself.

But these "moments" are *extremely* rare and fleeting, and I was not stupid. I knew seizing whatever combination of fake and real validation was happening around me was crucial. It ain't a brick house, the Palace. It's an ice sculpture. Grab all the fucking bacon-wrapped dates and 401(k)s and compliments while you can. Because regardless of what vocal fry Voldemort with an Android is insisting, it's all going to disappear from your life in a fucking second. And "OMG, who *are* you!" will fade back into ". . . *who* are you?"

Which I was ready for, and reminded myself every day was coming. I was just hoping I could cheat the system. Here's how. I'd use the ever-temporary, allowed-in-the-Palace phase to garner some sort of actor credit score. Then when I was inevitably found out and exiled, I'd still have *some* crumb of cachet. But a useful crumb. Perhaps enough to play a stern hospital administrator on a TBS show about goblins running a cancer ward. A lasting, secure, bill-paying job. And maybe one of the future-shiny preteen stars of that show will pull up an ancient Getty image of me squinting at a lotion gifting suite, and say, *Gee . . .* you *were in the Palace once?* And I'll say, *That was a long time ago, little Juniper Arrow Paltrow. Long time ago.*

This would also enable me to achieve the most difficult, insane actress feat possible. I loved acting and wanted to keep doing it until I died. Making faces through crow's feet and gesturing with wrinkled hands. For a good living. Forever. No expiration date. I can roll my eyes at the business all I want and pretend that it's all farce and no substance. But it's not. I still wanted all the things I wanted when I was four. I just knew now that the balls-showing emperor was the dude to pay for it.

So I tried.

I was advised to get a publicist and social media accounts. This was to commence the apparently necessary shaping of public-eye-actress narrative of *Hey, Ohio and Poland, I'm Betty, your girlfriend*. A mandatory world-seduction seemingly exclusive to actresses. Joaquin Phoenix can be grumbly and obscure, but even the shiniest of his female counterparts still has to play the seesaw of personality branding for the masses. Daniel Day-Lewis never has to tell a self-deprecating story in a bandage dress. (Although . . . someone, write this short film.)

But we've been over all this in the so-you're-an-actress essay. If that's still in the book. If this is still a book. I wonder if this will be a book? I'm going to keep writing and pretend it is.

I did the things. Well, not *all* the things. I got a publicist. I had Twitter for a second, but two mean comments and three compliments that sat the wrong way sent me into an emotional coma so embarrassing that I deleted my account. A misspelled dagger sentence about my fat ass and lack of talent from one 'roidy virgin in Canada was enough to drive me away from the internet forever. I don't know how actors handle it. Instagram was something I steered entirely clear of for both pat-myself-on-the-back reasons and aw-Betty-that's-sad reasons. Unpopular opinion but . . . I do think we will look back on this phase of duck-faced selfies and filters and feel horrified. The world burned while we posed. But the main reason for my Instagram aversion is my pitiful, afternoon-erasing face dysmorphia. Seeing pictures of myself rockets me to a sad, dark, dumb planet. Creating a public forum where the world could choose to *agree* with me felt like shooting therapy fish in a suicide barrel. (I'm still fully participating and contributing to an industry based on my own vanity, so my lack of posting pictures of myself is probably less evidence of being grounded and admirable and more hypocritical and deluded. I don't sleep well.)

Mostly I'm disappointed in the lingering story I tell myself. That all ambition and accomplishment is just 100 percent vanity. Especially in women, especially in myself. So every step forward in the name of rooting for myself, I have to cancel out with an act of look-away sabotage. Which makes me so sad that that's still how my brain works. So whether opting out of social media can be filed under priorities in the name of feminism or self-suppression in the name of antifeminism is for my already-oversuitcased therapist to unpack.

But still. It's confusing to me that to have a seat at the table, we have to sell all the things that shut us out of the conference room in the first place. Are we only allowed to wear the pants while our asses look good in them?

Try not to think about it too much, Gilpin. Just stuff your pockets with snacks and a mortgage before this ice sculpture melts and Zendaya asks for some ID.

There is a particular awards-show circuit that is a perfect snapshot of the Palace in all its glory. Its culmination is one of the shiniest nights in Hollywood, where teary starlets accept trophies in *Gone with the Wind* meets *Star Trek* drag. These trophies are granted by a particular body of judges. This group is relatively obscure to the public. I had always pictured them as a society of Tom Selleck-y–looking film savants, an esteemed group of entertainment connoisseurs. Maybe they quoted *Citizen Kane* over espresso, and could identify the inspiration of an opening tracking shot by the mimicked fractured light, making notes in their Moleskins that this director was the real deal because of *x*, or this actor deserved recognition for their soul-bloodshed in project *y*. Then together the quoting Sellecks would summit, pacing in Cary Grant suits through the night, wracked over which artist deserved what accolade, rewatching the pieces at hand on a loop to make sure they took every moment of genius into account. Then and only then were nominees and winners selected.

No, babe.

People are certainly recognized for good work. But the idea that *that's* the currency on which the Ribbon Contest is decided is a Santa Bunny fairy tale you better kiss goodbye.

For the first season of *GLOW,* I was advised to try for this specific trophy contest. I learned that attending a party hosted by this Tom Selleck troupe of talent sommeliers was the vital first step in garnering their attention. Surely there I would perform some sort of ceremonious handoff of a DVD, where maybe we'd guffaw over a cucumber sandwich, but then it was time for The Work to speak for itself, and off they'd go to a soundproof booth to delight in the subtleties of my choices in episode 4. Maybe I'd clink *one* celebratory glass with Judi Dench, but then it was early to bed for work the next day. Judi would understand—one wanted to rest up to emote at 5:00 a.m. instead of drinking gimlets with Lorde till dawn. The *art* is what gained Palace entry in the first place after all. Can't be hungover for its perpetuation, Judi!

Again no.

It became rapidly clear that attending a party as an actress, particularly *this* party, could not be less casual. Or . . . expensive. The people receiving the following funds are incredibly hardworking professionals, many of them brilliant and deserving. This is not an indictment of their worth or necessity to this business. On the contrary, they make it go round. Way fucking more than I do. I seek only to demonstrate how much thought and dollar and orchestration go into crafting the illusion of Actress at Party.

OK. To get into this particular party, you need a publicist to aggressively, passionately, campaign for you to get an invite. Which is . . . *very* expensive. One of the main goals of the party is to have your picture taken, where you have to look like a person whom the *party* begged to come, not the other way around. Not an unknown actress in an Airbnb with one fork and dirty Old Navy laundry, but a trillionaire pop star graciously stopping by even though you're jet-lagged from Minsk. So I met with a stylist. She fit me with fabrics I didn't know existed, the equivalent of caviar in thread form, tailored and torqued to my body, sculpting the lie that the outfit was a mere glimpse into my real closet. One styling fee is also . . . many dollars. I hired a professional hair stylist and makeup artist, knowing that without them I would arrive with wet hair and five visible zits. I paid the (again, deserved) hundreds to these illusionists to curl and blush me out of Eliza Doolittle–dom.

All in hopes that the mysterious Sellecks would consider me for a trophy. For a price tag that totaled over twice my rent. I was not in a position to spend twice my rent on one cocktail party. But I was also not in a position to wait for the next lightning strike. Not when I'd gone bolt-less for so long.

The night of the event I also paid for a nice car, suddenly horrified that Will or Grace would see me exit a soiled Uber Prius and notify the Palace guards. In said car, I noticed my snugly sewn please-like-me dress was tugging downward, making suffocated pierogi shapes out of my armpit skin. Now that I was not standing upright in a fitting room, my thighs were voicing their discomfort with the Twiggy fit of the dress by turning a troubling purple. Grasping at control-straws, I powdered my face in the pitch-dark back seat, then remembered the makeup artist had warned me *not* to powder.

The second I stepped out of the car I screamed. My calves seized like a cement rat was being electrocuted inside them. Since I had only posed stationary and afraid in these shoes, my muscles now reacted to walking two steps in torture sticks passing as stilettos. In the short walk from the curb to my waiting publicist, my gait went from wounded fawn to Jack Sparrow on a waterbed. Not quite the Gisele *I've arrived* stomp I'd promised the stylist.

I joined the line to the red carpet. This line is always a silly shock for such an event. You've spent hours pumping your ego with Cinderella-moment anxiety, whipping yourself into the idea that you are a cocainey princess about to explode into a Validation Derby. This is *your* night! Surely the night will begin with a cannon exploding you into a purple-lit room full of ex-boyfriends and journalists screaming your name, a tornado of shrieking compliments over a brass band that somehow got the sheet music to the songs you wrote in eighth grade, which . . . actually? Are *amazing*! But instead of a montage of Sexy Fast, you enter a slog of Slow Gross. The line to the red carpet is where you slowly realize that contrary to what you were told, this is *not* your night. It is not you entering your wedding, glowing and important, but crashing someone else's sweet sixteen, old and weird. You have to quickly erase your bridal butterflies compelling you to maniacally twirl, and instead . . . quietly stand, shuffling on fluorescent asphalt, exchanging tight smiles with *Grey's Anatomy* porn statues. The line is a long, awkward tonal shift—as if you were about to orgasm and a grandparent came in with a W-2. You stand two by two in a strange Noah's ark prom, sequined actor by blazered publicist, both anxious to trade the hair-tucking "ums" for bass-booming "whats?" inside.

I used this twenty-five minutes of DMV by *TMZ* to trouble-shoot. I tried my best to address the various choked flesh rolls bubbling out of my ever shrinking/sinking dress. I wanted to ask my publicist if it looked to *her* like my body was eating the fab-ric for dinner, but the poor woman was busy trying (as out-of-earshot as she could, bless her) to explain to the photographers who I was. Their faces twisted like she had informed them the chef was swapping their fillet with feces. I shook it off. After half an hour of a mental rabbit hole of bank statements and a scarring *Kiss Me Kate* high school menstrual memory, I exploded back into the present moment. I had reached the front.

OK, Betty. Take your moment. Enjoy this!

I stepped onto the carpet. Immediately: screams. Not of adora-tion, but . . . *rage.* Incredulous opposing shrieks for looking right no left, forward no back, smile don't smile, let's see some shoul-der EW *FUCK* YOUR SHOULDER, all in about three seconds. I heard maybe four clicks with blinding flash, my face frozen in a midsneeze where-am-I, my legs in a fell-from-a-balcony, pigeon-toed apology.

Take a breath. Do the pose and face you've seen in the pedicure mag-azines. Relax.

I breathed. I posed. I smized.

But no, suddenly no more clicks, now in silent unison they're waving me right, down down down to the . . . next photogra-phers? No. It's over.

That was it.

My publicist met me in my shell shock at the tattered carpet's end, her eyes flicking open wide for a second, taking in my dress.

"Before we go in, just gonna . . ."

She did her best to undo the carnal wrongs of my body. We watched together as she tried to fix my armpit overflow, her two fingers prodding the suffocated gnome-labia that the fabric choked my skin into. She fixed an apparently elaborate lip-gloss error that I told myself wouldn't show up in pictures. Nor would the aforementioned GL. Or the open-mouthed terror in my painted face.

Once inside, I shook my head into a reset. Here we go! I scanned excitedly for the Sellecks. I deep-inhaled into my role for the evening: a gracious, well-spoken actor who treats compliments as little conversation openers into craft and theory. I'd be patient with each member of the committee, assuring them everyone gets a turn.

You see where this is going.

The committee did not want to talk to me. But . . . the committee?

The committee was . . . insane. You guys. They. Are. Insane.

Picture your most unstable aunt. Picture your most problematic gym teacher and give him an accent and a pashmina. Picture a cross-eyed, doll-collecting sea captain.

I had *one* actual conversation with *one* of them. Who very sweetly pretended to have seen *GLOW.* We exchanged a few sentences about the spicy tuna. When a cast member from *The Big Bang Theory* walked in, she sobbed. A person I waved to, for no reason, or my arm was trying to abandon me. The teary committee member gaped. *"Do you know them? Introduce me!!"*

I realized I could be terrible or brilliant in episode 4. It didn't matter for this pageant. But if I only knew *Sheldon* . . .

She soon extricated herself from my pauses, scurrying after a passing *Ocean's 11* Adonis in sneakers with no time. My publicist made a "let's try again!" face. Then followed a very sad twenty minutes. Guiding me by the elbow, she circled me around the perimeter of the club in silence, like I was a blind cow up for auction, but we'd gotten the county fair time wrong, and besides, no one wanted the cow with a low star meter. I drank a few sips of a drink inspired by a miniseries about cannibals. I had a four-second conversation in line for the bathroom with a talented Australian about hating ourselves, but then they were pulled away for a picture, for which I helpfully stepped aside and into a small indoor tree, whose branches gave me a little hug that hit too close to home.

So home I went.

Two rents poorer.

Listen, my time in the Palace wasn't all horrors and soul-selling. A lot of it was . . . fun. I danced an embarrassing contradiction, rolling my eyes in disdain at the value system, then in the next breath begging that system for approval. But it was hard not to get a little drunk on the juice they were pouring. Especially after decades of a lot of . . . sad Gilpin. Ribby and teary in my high school dorm, or high and lonely in a car with a higher driver, or avoiding eye contact with the mirror because I hated my face, or hearing and reading and saying *no* over and over again until it felt like *yes* was a myth. Feeling pretty in a dress with a group of other dresses laughing at your joke *feels* like yes, even if it's bought.

I never made it to the level where you don't have to buy the *yes,* if that level even exists. But I was going to seize the high before it ran out. I was like Meg March when she loses herself for a night dancing in borrowed lipstick and a loaner gown. I was also Jo March, arms folded on the sidelines, disgusted at her sister's foolishness. I tried to ignore her. This was all going to poof and be gone, anyway. I was Cinderella at 11:58, snorting a huge line with the prince's hot valet in the bathroom.

Fuck it. Muffle your conscience and dance before your glass shoe explodes.

18

RUN

The line I straddled felt drastic and like a secret. I played the part of Glittery I Made It while doing the necessary treading of shark waters to stay there. I did talk shows and carpets and podcasts where I mimed Betty of Comfort and Luxury but was still self-taping on my bathroom floor for any job possible. Most of any incoming paycheck was spent perpetuating the illusion of needing no more paychecks. Fable-wise, I was trying to be both bugs: gathering shit for the cave for winter *and* partying before the snow came. Winter being the world getting tired of me and no more claps. But somehow it felt like I was failing at both—the cave was empty and the party wasn't fun.

But stability and ecstasy were both *imminent,* surely.

Career-wise I was at a sort of actress (salad) fork in the road. The things I was auditioning for pointed at two different versions of a career, as actress roles for one's thirties do. Occasionally I would audition for "sexy lead in *x*," but mostly "frazzled mother in *z*." I could feel the business mulling over whether I was still fetal enough to hold a gun in the front or if I'd curdled into having a teenage daughter in the back. I played the mother of an actress *eight* years younger than me. Most of my male peers wouldn't play fathers of infants for another decade.

I didn't care. I tried for and did any and every job they'd let me on the grounds to do. Some great and some that my actor friends tried to hide their "wait but *why*" reactions to. I wrote letters begging for jobs they turned their nose up at. They didn't understand. It wasn't *Vogue* covers and Oscars I was after; that would be insane. It was something else.

I was *almost there*. The thing just around the corner that would rewrite my ending. The curse waiting for me, where I stare into soapsuds in stillness, where all the neglected Salem demons finally catch up with me. And swallow me whole. Banish me to drawstring depression, cowering from bake sale inquiries and lifting an invisible boulder off my chest every morning before forcing myself out of bed. Somewhere in this high of flights and lashes and sixteen-hour workdays of emoting in Spanx *had* to be the antidote. The fix that would put enough distance between me and the waiting dark.

And if that was impossible, maybe frantically rowing while the tide was in would be enough. If it was inevitable that my final act was Emily Dickinson Sighs in Sweats, maybe it would be enough to know I'd tried. And then once the phone stopped ringing in six months or three years, I'd just turn and accept it. The Persephone trailing me all this time, the self waiting to pull me under the covers back into hiding and hating the mirror. In a parallel universe, I would wake up furious with myself that I hadn't fought it for a while, or had missed the moment. I didn't want that universe to be *this* one. I was terrified of *me* being the reason I didn't happen. I didn't want my own blood on my hands.

So I ran. As fast as I could.

For a decade of our relationship, I did a lot of sitting. Upside-down sighing on the couch, folding paper cranes out of old magazines, waiting for Cosmo to finish a conference call so we could order Szechuan. I walked Babe all over Brooklyn, superstitiously turning left not right in an attempt to trigger my phone to ring with a job. But I was around, all the time. And that was really lovely. Waiting, yes, but also mostly laughing through ice cream, holding the boy and the furry one through Sunday crosswords. Finagling discounts for theatre tickets with friends to see whatever other friend was in that show, then shoveling risotto balls and martinis in each others' faces while we waxed hyperbolic over her moment in act 2. Then maybe an off-season Christmas carol at 2:00 a.m. waiting in sundresses for the C train. Women the world told me were my rivals who were now my family. I got to see them all the time.

Now suddenly I was never home. Ever. In one year I took over fifty flights. Every job I took was across the world somewhere impossibly far away. Film schedules are built around the star needing to be elsewhere yesterday, to don prosthetic Oscar noses or wine-taste with Tom Brady. So as Friend's Wife #2 or Unhinged Exposition Neighbor, I would work one or two days a week, otherwise required to wander alone for weeks in whatever nondescript Soviet Cleveland location we shot in. They were all small parts in OK movies. I was elated to be working, but it was strange. The *acting* part I always loved, no matter how low the future Rotten Tomatoes score. What they don't tell you is that the *acting* part makes up *maybe* 5 percent of the time. The rest is . . . shockingly . . . lonely. So many solo cheap sushis doing the online crossword billions of miles away from anyone I knew. So much *Bachelorette* in beige and sterile hotel rooms. Failed FaceTime attempts with friends in opposite time zones. Bunching pillows against me to mimic the shapes of a lumber-jack and small beast to crowd me into sleep. Cosmo would visit when he could, watching football in a Marriott alone un-til I burst in at dawn covered in makeup and grime, good for twenty minutes of one-syllable conversation until I passed out in my room service broth. When I went home, it was only for a few sleepless days at a time, unpacking and repacking my suitcase without it ever leaving the center of our living room. Once when I told him on the phone the "good news" that after Atlanta and New Orleans I'd go right to Vancouver before To-ronto, Cosmo asked after a sigh, "When's the part where we get to be married?"

One such rushed, forced, horrible two-day laundry-and-one-kiss trip I will never forget: I had just wrapped a horror movie where I played a woman panicked about her "geriatric pregnancy." (I was thirty-one at the time.) I flew home to hold Cosmo and Babe for two days, hoping it would be like plugging into a wall charger of You're Okay and Loved before I was gone again. I was about to leave for four months, off to film *Wuther-ing Heights* in London. Sorry—did I say *Wuthering Heights* in London? I meant *A Dog's Purpose 2* in Winnipeg. To play a severe alcoholic failed lounge singer/terrible mother in a dog movie. Sorry—did I say a dog movie? I meant a dog movie . . . sequel. My character's main trait was the hatred of . . . dogs. And children. And joy. The schedule had me working one day a week but needed me in . . . Winnipeg . . . for the entirety of the four-month shoot. On days off I was free to take in the sights of tundra-ed . . . Winnipeg.

While I tearily repacked my suitcase in Brooklyn, Babe came over to snarf disapprovingly into my toiletries, as was his wont. Then, slowly and almost comically, he started sinking. His back legs drifted away from each other on the wood floor, settling splayed in a canine Elvis split. Laughing a little, I propped him back up. But again he sank. I called Cosmo over and we shuffled quietly, watching this slow farce, unsure whether it was supposed to be funny or not. *Maybe he tore something sprinting through the park in one of his "Jason Bourne eats pigeon" fantasies,* we thought. We'll take him to the vet Monday to make sure. Oh right, *you* will take him. I'll be doing . . . the dog movie.

Sequel.

The basic plot of the dog movie is that dogs get reincarnated. Which is a lovely thought. But it also means that in the movie, the dog dies. Like . . . seven times. The same voice-over greets you in the new dog, but still. You've watched the last dog *die*. And this one will, too, and so on. As a dog lover, I saw this as emotional terrorism to the highest degree. There were parts of the script I just never read because I couldn't see the page through rage-tears. But in Winnipeg I bit my tongue. This paycheck was more than fifty plays' worth. I shut my mouth and screamed at the beagle on *action* like a good girl.

Even though I'd achieved a semblance of Palace entry, I knew where I stood. The internal hierarchy listed me as a human penny. It was strange: I was *so* much further in my career than I ever thought I'd get. But the closer I was to success made me panic about failure way more than when I was making *literal* pennies. Things that I would once consider a huge *yes* I filed as tiny *almosts*. Back when my rent was low and my schedule was flightless, I felt much more satisfied than I did once I started grabbing brass rings. I never worried more about money than when I started having a little. I never rolled my eyes at my own resume more than when I finally had one.

I was also pretty convinced that in terms of a dramatic film role, the dog movie (sequel) would be the ceiling for me. Which is nothing to sneeze at; I just didn't love the story my brain was telling me. *The ice sculpture is melting, you idiot. Excommunication is nigh. So you're missing a friend's wedding—you'll make the next one. Emote in Winnipeg before you're defrauded tomorrow.*

So I tried to shoehorn in my Blanche Hamlet experience to a movie where the real Hamlet was a St. Bernard. I overacted to a mezzanine that didn't exist, sobbing in scenes that didn't require tears, while . . . um . . .

On my, uh . . . my shoulders?

Sat . . .

. . . turkey.

Slices of turkey, reader. For . . .

(Type it out, Betty. You can do this.)

For the pug's eyeline.

Like raw flesh epaulets on my character's mohair robe, honey-baking into my memory, ensuring I'd never *really* sleep again. If I may? Turkey on one's shoulders for sobbing scenes takes a piece of you away forever. And so we roast on, breasts against the current, basted back ceaselessly into the PTSD.

Valiantly, I filmed on. I screamed shaky monologues at my human scene partners, one of whom had white baby food smeared on their lips like upsetting culinary erotica. They were smeared so, of course, to motivate the basset hound to run toward them. Away from *me,* evil incarnate. Whimpering in horror. I did a scene where I had to scream (*scream*) in the face (in the FACE) of a tiny . . . beagle . . . puppy. Reader? A puppy. I was encouraged by the director in a whisper to "really go for it." A whisper unfortunately only I could hear, so the ensuing Cruella Dahmer behavior looked like it was my idea alone. After the first take, the puppy wrangler asked me through tears to pull it back.

"Do you . . . not . . . like dogs?"

The thought of Babe, basically my son, thousands of miles away with a mysterious leg condition shut down my brain and liquefied my heart. Not wanting to erupt in a Greek wail at work, I offered a curt, neutral response, which gave the unintentional impression that *yes, it's true: I hate dogs.*

In these weeks and months away I missed big, devastating, why-wasn't-I-there moments, searing regrets on my calendar that still keep me up at night. Cosmo is a man to the mannest degree. I've watched him chainsaw and burn and axe his way through wilderness, picking up snakes and goddamn porcupines and hawks with his bare hands, seen him smash through drywall and drink five gasoliney whiskeys without blinking. But when it comes to Babe, his boy, Cosmo is a boy himself, weeping in overalls at the kindergarten door, as Cosmo's mom told me he'd done in 1982. While I screamed at poodles in Canada, Cosmo held Babe through vet appointments that filled the weeks, trying to understand why our dog's legs were deciding to quit us. I should have been there, and I wasn't.

The answer came over the phone to me late at night, Cosmo's voice shaking and pausing for ten and twelve horrible Mississippis between words. Babe basically had ALS for dogs. It meant a slow, inevitable paralysis, starting with his back legs and creeping its way horribly to his perfect chiseled block of a circus warrior head. Could be two years, could be months. But eventually. The thing we all pretend won't happen. *So* much sooner than we'd ever thought. We had had him for ten years. In our heads, he would outlive the redwoods he'd peed on.

I got off the phone earlier than I should have. But well, I had a big scene in the morning.

I had to make alcoholic amends to a bichon frise.

It was my character's redeeming soliloquy, a time jump forty years ahead. I was put in elaborate old-age prosthetics: a turkey neck and crinkly face. These made me look less like a Caucasian grandmother, and more troublingly like a caramelized turtle's foreskin, appearing in cashmere to narrate a horror movie. I scream-sobbed into a frazzled cupcake dog, a dog that, impossibly, had "the Rachel" haircut. My eyeline to my human scene partner was blocked by said cupcake's ribbon-dancer-wielding wrangler, flailing violently next to the deadpan sound guy, a sound guy *praying* for death, both people just trying to do their jobs near an actress milking a proverbial cat in a very much literal dog movie. When the cameras were facing me, my performance was terrible—God awful, unforgivably bad acting. When we turned around for Bella McJangles's coverage for the hamburger gag, I shouted my lines from tiptoes on a folding chair, miles from being in the frame. It was my only good take of the day.

I called Cosmo on the ride back to my hotel, but the time difference had put the boys to bed hours ago. I slept on my closed fist that night, to mimic someone holding my hand.

THE CHANCE

I still loved alpha women. But now my friendships were equal and communicative and my fucking lifeblood. But, to a person, they still seemed so much braver than me. I was shocked that my actress friends had the courage to say "no thanks" to a job if they didn't like it. Outwardly I wrote their choosiness off as foolish. *Who the hell are you to be so sure something better is coming along? We ain't that special. Reaching for the stars is for illiterate narcissists!* Secretly I felt wildly jealous of their surety of worth. Then quietly and tinily I would hope for things that felt so far away. When the rare Huge Opportunity came along, I would let my heart leap for a second, let my brain take three shaky steps down a *what if* road. But protectively, Shame and Shrug would sweep in to remind me how unrealistic it would be. That maybe even if we got the job, we'd get there and . . . maybe the tiny light wouldn't come out at all.

So I did things that break my heart to think about. In the waiting room of Callback for Big Movie, I meant to go pee and then I just . . . kept walking, to the stairwell, and onto the street, and a

Camel Light and twenty blocks later it was safer than their telling *me* no. In a voice lesson to prepare for Big Oscar-y Movie Musical Audition, the piano guy made a face like "eek" at one of the notes I hit, or rather didn't, and I thought, *Oh God you're right,* and I cancelled the audition. Or I'd focus all my prep time on trying to cover the parts of my face I hated, and accidentally on purpose underprepare the big scene that would actually win the job. Of course there were far more that I tried in earnest to get and simply didn't for all the normal reasons. But it was the ones I took away from myself that keep me up at night. Why did I do that? If it was meant as protection, why did it hurt so much? If I was running all the time at this mystery achievement that would solve everything . . . why did it feel like sinking into glue instead of whipping through wind?

Then one time it was different.

It is a long, intricate, probably boring, and irrelevant story. Certainly meaningless in the timeline of the world. I'll leave out most of it. Let's have martinis if you're interested in the details. But to me it meant so much, for all the opposite reasons I thought it would.

A director friend called me. I had worked with him on an episode of Betty-makes-too-many-faces-as-guest-star-and-has-to-be-edited-around, aka my Zorro "Z."

"I'm sending you a script for a big movie that I want you to be the lead in. It's really good. Betty. You'd be a movie star."

Fool.

I reminded this dunce that movie math didn't let women without shampoo contracts or problematic fan sites be the lead in

studio movies. Did he mean a different part? Was there a disapproving woman with a dish towel? A nippled encourager who
gets eaten?

"No, no, I know! Exactly. It's a fake-out. I'll cast a bunch of big
names for the characters who die at the beginning. And we'll just
have the trailer be only them. So the audience doesn't see you
coming at all. We'll trick them into you being the lead!"

It was an insanely sweet thought. But I knew this poor, talented
man was mistaken. He would still have to fight ruthlessly for a
non–pop star to play whatever part this was, a battle he would
lose. Going from blackout drunk corgi-punting grandmother in
Doggie Dies 2 to major lead in whatever this fancy movie was just
wasn't going to happen. Reluctantly, I read the script.

It was a funny, violent genre movie about America's current
state of fuckery: an Ivy League thesis statement wrapped in a
fart-joke roast of 2019 America. All encased in an action movie. I
laughed out loud at the parts I agreed with and winced in recognition at the digs at my side of the aisle. Then thirty pages in, the
lead character entered. And my heart sank like a moose fainting
in slow motion.

At the center of this bloody and smart and silly script was a
woman who had given up on herself. She was a sort of walking
shell, traumatized and over it, middle finger in the sky, making
crazy *the fuck cares* eyes at the world around her, waiting in a smirk
for the day when the curse inside her would eat her whole. But
I saw in her strangeness that there was something brewing in
her monosyllables. A tiny, forbidden, suffocated part of her waving through the blackness, a centimeter tall. Thinking, illegally,
*Maybe. Fucking probably not but maybe. Maybe the darkness that takes
over my Saturdays and churning electricity behind my eyes that unsettles*

neighbors, maybe just once that could be funneled into something . . .
magnificent. Maybe just once in this life I keep insisting I don't care
about . . . the tiny light will come out, into the room, and mean some-
thing.

I sat at my computer in my Winnipeg beige hotel cube, closed
my computer, and sobbed. Because that was it. Of course it's exactly what I felt, what I wanted more than anything. I knew there
was no wizard, I knew the Palace was a joke. But I did still think
there was a chance there was something in me that I wanted to
extricate. Something I did not want to die with. This part was the
chance.

So, of course:

I wrote an email to the director saying no. "Sorry, but no. I
won't be able to audition for this. The Dog Movie is too demand-
ing, and also my arm feels weird lately, and this weekend I actually have to get my thyroid medication at a pharmacy that's pretty
far away but I need the walk. And most of all, dude, thank you
but . . . it's just not going to happen. So let's not break our own
hearts on purpose."

Then my hand turned into a stranger's, and I hit delete. And I
typed "let's try."

I taped my phone to the window of my Winnipeg hotel room
and did the audition scene a thousand times with my own re-
corded voice reading the other lines. I made the fucking tape. I
deleted every take. The stranger's hand went to my phone's trash
and undeleted one and sent it.

Two weeks later I got a phone call that made me sit down on
frozen Canadian pavement.

I got the job.

On a break from *Citizen Canine,* I flew home. I babbled to Cosmo my disbelief and fear and excitement—this was *it*. Can you fucking believe this is actually happening? Cosmo patted my hair with one hand and Babe's fur with the other, the beast harrumphing from the back seat. I buzzed to the boys through Babe's water-therapy appointment, Babe fumbling ridiculously on an underwater tread-mill, eyes darting between us asking who's fucking idea was this.

In theatre, there was always an emphasis on letting go of the re-sult. That the second you focus on the presentation of the thing, you will ruin the very thing you're trying to present. The purpose of work is the work itself, the fleeting moment where you touch something true. Then it's gone and you leave it behind. It's not really your business if the world likes it or not.

This line of thinking was easier to follow when the "result" was a handful of other stoned friends watching your monologue in In-tro to Shapes, or when the grannies in row B got up during your curtain call in what for a second looked like a standing ovation but was actually them just . . . leaving. But then who cares, in an hour you're spending your tiny paycheck on group fries, in tears laughing at the fumbled knife prop, and tomorrow's good show erases tonight's bomb. When triumphs and failures felt smaller, they were also for free. It was easy to focus on the part I loved, then let it go, not looking back to see if the world approved.

Now things were different. More eyes and voices were weigh-ing in. The Palace pointing at the clock. My own brain doing the same. And of course, a new cacophony of executioners suddenly vital to one's career; the horrors of the *internet*. I envy my parents' generation of actors where outside opinions were exclusively on parchment. Approval or distaste appeared a few times in print, but then was forgotten once those leaflets hit the trash. Now actors' sock and grammar and character choices are the internet's raw meat. In the terrifying universe of trial-by-comments section, pedestals are far too high and the guillotines absurdly sharp. Certain achievements get actors worship that should be reserved for nurses and soldiers. Then their falters earn condemnation appropriate for kitten murderers. In my year of panic-posing in ruffles and folding arms in costumed cardigans, I got caught up in fearing these voices. I was terrified to learn that this fear made the actual *acting* part harder. The sacred stuff, the part I loved. It became more and more difficult to achieve that internal placidity where ideas and risks could float to the surface. Easier and easier to worry about my place in the world instead of what I had to say about being there.

I was doing all this stage-momming on behalf of my own childhood dream without realizing the kid herself was slowly disappearing.

But *this* job was different. This role was different. I'm not saying it was Hamlet—it was just . . . I could feel it happening, the thing I never thought would. A disabling of all the self-hate hurdles and roadblocks and body shame and fear. A clear highway for the tiny light, an unblocked path from its dungeon out my mouth to the world. I needed to do this part.

Some weird spell happened where I let go. I dove all the way in preparing the character, creativity doors flying open in my brain that I'd feared were sealed shut. I wrote pages and pages of what I saw as the women in *her* brain, shaking in disbelief that I was going to be allowed to do this, bursting with readiness to get to the first day of being her.

––––

Then the God of Logistics had a good laugh at me and my little triumph narrative. Months and years of my life as an actor had been free, conflictless, thumb-twiddling, and available on the sofa. But now my phone rang with news that first made me laugh, then lie down for death. The boring stuff out of the way: the dates for season 3 of *GLOW* and the start of the movie overlapped. By one week. Legally, apparently, this was a nonnegotiable, unfixable problem. A few weeks of scary phone calls between suits happened. But then I got that final call saying Betty, it's over. It can't work.

You have to let this one go.

In the peak of my stoner years, I would play a dumb game. It was an exercise in bloodshot futility, as it required functioning long-term memory. For those who live here, New York is a relatively small grid of land mines of your past. You turn a corner with headphones and suddenly the curve of a building or chipped blue on a door has you in sobs. *This is where you choked a goodbye to him, this is where you puked on her, this is where the guy with the biggest no-teeth smile hopped your hopscotch.* Squinty and tie-dyed, I would often try to wave through time at future me. *Remember this.* Here you are outside your Houston Street apartment: wave. Wave across the street at wrinkled you waving back, in the future, showing your kids where you used to live. The problem is I never remembered the whens and wheres of the waves. The odds of my seventy-year-old self suddenly recalling stoned teen me's coordinates to share a quantum powwow were not likely.

But here, teary and helpless on my Winnipeg bed, sobbing into flannel like an unstable woodcutter, I suddenly felt . . . a wave.

Of sorts. Some vague minuscule echo—me from the future, waving back at me through the years and . . . watching.

I know I am metaphor-y and insane. But like . . . fuck ghosts, and astrology, and *The Secret* and, honestly, acupuncture. I'm telling you—something was fucking watching me. Uh. *I* was watching me.

I picked up the phone.

". . . Tell them . . . um . . . tell them . . ."

Here we go, I guess.

"Tell them no."

". . . What? That's not . . . that's not how it works. It's over. I'm sorry."

"No I know but just um."

Me watching me.

". . . No. Is *my* answer."

I think it just finally got old. Casting myself as the cowering supporting character in someone else's swelling epic. Especially if suddenly some haunted Me was watching to see what I'd do. Whoever this bitch was, I didn't want to disappoint her. For once, I would not let myself stand in my own way. The brainwomen who insisted they were protecting me now looked like glaring examples of Munchausen by proxy. *Go,* said the once-mouse. *If this is my one tiny light chance, then please go.* Or rather, *Get. The fuck. Out of my way.*

Because I need to push the fucking elevator button.

I started to write.

With no sanity or plan, I got the email addresses of all the Dudes in Charge. Dudes whose jobs did not involve the intricacies of an unknown puppet's scheduling conflicts or childhood dreams. Dudes who say, "What else?" at the head of glass conference tables and ruffle Leo's hair over foam sushi 'cause they're that close. Dudes who run the Palace. It was like a hair elastic emailing the sun for a favor. But I did.

I wrote emails. I wrote . . . essays. Addled E. E. Cummings wedding toasts, like Evita going to the balcony and sob-screaming a college essay to the masses. I emailed the Palace kings and said, "Sirs, picture it. Picture a girl with a dream."

I wrote them about watching my parents from the wings, about my little life of trying. That in a business where you are lucky to get one chance, I felt that this one was mine. I sat back from the computer in disbelief. Who was this person fighting for herself? This . . . protagonist?

The replies came back. Amusing sentence structure, but I'm sorry. We can't.

There was one final name of people to beg—the sole woman on the list. Since I had been terrified of alpha women my whole life until I learned they were life's secret, it was lamely no surprise that appealing to *her* was my last resort. I apparently still had some femme-fear to conquer. My email to her began:

"I'm tempted to spend six paragraphs convincing you that I'm a sort of quiet pajamas mouse person who isn't insane and is terrified to ask for the salt, let alone a favor from my boss. But without sounding too dramatic, I do feel like this is a moment I will look back on for the rest of my life. I'm terrified it will be with regret. So I'm tasing the Aunt Lydia at the door to my brain and asking for your help."

I puked up my story.

Within an hour, my inbox dinged.

"Thank you for the note. I am glad to hear from you, and always respect and admire an empowered woman who expresses what she wants. I can't promise anything, except that I am digging more into it myself."

Weeks later I learned that she stayed on a long conference call listing why-nots, and patiently waded through repeated we-can'ts, until at last, an . . . ugh-fine.

I was half bluffing the empowerment bulldozer. As in so many other times in my life, I needed another woman to actually pull the lever for me. As Marie did. As Bunny did. As Margot and Lela and Dani and blue- and brown-eyed former rivals did. And now as this woman did.

(Cindy Holland. Thank you.)

So: I did the movie. It was called *The Hunt*.

The self-worth bluff lasted longer than I expected. Preparing for the movie, I wrote billion-word paragraphs of ideas. I trained every day, not to look tiny, but strong. I was playing a veteran. I wanted to look like an unnerving warrior. In the past, my "job preparation" involved crash-dieting and self-sabotage. If I had *x* amount of time before day one, I would spend it thinking about how I was going to fuck all this up with bad acting or jiggly thighs. *Don't bother trying to make this special*. This time, no. Fuck no. Now I was apparently pretending to be a woman with confidence and a plan. I changed up the process for this job. By the time we started shooting, I had ten journals spilling with her thoughts. Day one in the trailer mirror, I laughed at my reflection. My shoulders that were once glued to my ears in a silent *I'm sorry,* arms only existing to carry the queen's books, could now deadlift two hundred pounds.

OK, one last lame little victory to share. Before it all exploded so spectacularly in catastrophe.

Filming was fun. OK it was . . . so, so, *so* much fun. It was mostly me making insane, INSANE faces (when you have a thing you have a thing) and making gore-confetti of the bad guys. A lot of thousand-yard-stares into sudden sprinting. But mentally, it felt like I had entered a different universe. I wasted no brain-time on hating my face—I barely wore any makeup on-screen, a career first. There was no problematic, confusing flirtation dynamic to soak up valuable idea time—instead lots of professional *Good-morning* nods and then immediately into the work at hand. Instead of feeling like an aging, pudgy courtesan asking permission to be there, I felt . . . valued, and calm. And free.

And because of that feeling, I did my really weird ideas. All of them. Usually I'd just half do one or two. But here in this intensely strange movie, I did them all. I fought this hard to get here—I wasn't going to disappoint the Watcher now. I let the director (the fucking genius Craig Zobel) in on said weird ideas and to my shock he completely understood them, often calling from his headset, "OK, Betty let's do a baby dinosaur take," our shorthand for the character's pure demented id. Something I thought that as a Barbie person I'd never, ever be allowed to baldly play. Something I'd watched male scene partners have piles of on the page while I writhed with dish-toweled jealousy. Now I had no fake lashes and no boundaries. Guys, I'm not saying it or I was good. I'm just saying it *felt* good. It felt spectacular.

In one particular scene, I promised myself I'd ask for a free take, one where I could improvise an idea I had.

It's a turn in the movie where the character realizes her moment has come. It's a fork in the road—everyone's dead but her, she's the last man standing. She's the only person who can kill the bad guy. She has two choices. She can say, *Fuck this* and walk away, returning to a life of shrugging through a darkness that was eating her alive. She can keep insisting there will never be The Moment for her and let it pass her by. Or she can say, *Yep. There is something in me that is fucking insane, the thing I thought was my albatross but maybe today could be my jetpack. Maybe I can harness this inner hum into magnificence. For one day. Maybe I can use that hum to kill this psychopath.*

And *maybe I, Betty, could use mine, too.*

So I did my weird idea. I improvised a little, and nonsensically mimed something along those lines. Her naming this very thing. A half-Muppet, half-witch moment, perhaps fodder for editing-room ridicule, but very thoroughly *me*. Six-year-old ham me, seventeen-year-old dark me, future old me, all the *me*s. Exactly what I wanted to do, exactly how I wanted to do it. Who knew if they'd actually use it—that felt beside the point. I had done the specific thing I never thought I'd get to do. Even if it was just for the boom mic guy and the cutting-room floor.

Back at my hotel that night, I jumped on the bed like I was kicking the shit out of an enemy and slapped the ceiling every time like it was the sky and I was Zeus.

But let's remember: the problem with your American dream coming true is that it comes true . . . in America.

Once we wrapped, a different narrative arose around me doing this movie that was hard not to listen to. The voices from my iPhone seemed to think this movie would *drastically* change my life Palace-wise. That its release would explode me into a parade of ease and praise. No more crying in parking lots. I was assured we were weeks away from gowns and compliments and Scorsese where there had been auditions and begging and dog sequels. Soon, soon, my once-unwanted pale ass would be spray-tanned and full of smoke.

And then.

Ohhh, reader. And *then*.

"The shit hit the fan" *almost* covers it, if you T-shirt-gunned an Olympic pool's worth of manure into a wind turbine over a nude beach. If we're going with that imagery, then, yes:

The shit hit the fan.

The political satire of *The Hunt* was both perfectly and horrifically timed. Apocalypse-calendar-wise, it was both the exact movie the nation needed, and the worst thing possible.

In the weeks leading up to the movie's release, America was going through one of its many nation-shits-its-pants months. Our trailer came out. It erroneously sold our satire as sincere. The already-mad-at-everything internet *exploded*. Misinformation around what the movie was *actually about* erupted into modern-day boos; thousands of misspelled . . . death threats. At everyone involved with the movie. And at me.

Thousands.

As promised, my face was *everywhere*. But not in a serum campaign or best-dressed collage. Instead it was plastered across dueling news channels. My face, guys. Normally screaming in opposition, the channels were now at last in harmonious agreement on one thing: that this poison suck-movie starring this unknown suck-actress was a national disgrace in film form. One of said channels who specialize in lying and screaming got my cell phone number and left messages asking about the nation's future. A theatre major falls in a forest.

This was all based on the world seeing the trailer. I assured myself that we just had to breathe through this phase of the internet wildly misrepresenting a movie *no one had actually seen,* then when the movie actually came *out,* we'd all have a therapeutic group laugh about how ironically wrong they'd been. It was a movie *literally about* Americans on Twitter getting it wrong and turning a joke into something dangerous. And that's what was *happening.* It all felt like a disturbing meta advertising campaign. But saying that out loud would be the bad word: a *spoiler.* And pour gasoline on death threats. We sat on our hands. The vitriol grew louder every day.

Then, it happened.

In an unprecedented, holy-shit move, the Dudes in Charge decided they were willing to lose a few million to put out this septic fire. They announced that the movie's release was cancelled. As in, it would never, ever come out.

Ever.

I was now in the strange situation of my dumb little personal opus being in jail, like your masterpiece paragraph being page 73 of a banned book. Helpless and pacing, I wrote an essay. A sample:

"The movie is about an internet falsehood that became a tidal wave in an Orwellian climate, which then silenced a group of people. And then in real life, the content of the movie became an internet falsehood that became a tidal wave in an Orwellian climate, which then silenced a group of people. And that, baby, is when satire will save us all." I of course included complicated, hard-to-follow metaphors, self-deprecation, and tit jokes. *Surely, I thought, an apologizey think piece will heal the nation and save my Big Moment.*

I was emailed a pat on the head. I was asked to "wait to publish for when we need it" (place it in a kiln). I was put into deflection media training. In a windowless boardroom on a studio lot, a sweating, bow-tied man peppered me with practice questions. He offered tweaks to my answers that would paint the studio as the hero. When I began an answer with a rope analogy, he interrupted with a hand up: "No metaphors." Dear, sweet God. I was not in baby dinosaur Kansas anymore.

I was on many calls with terrified voices instructing me to evade and extinguish, voices that *days* before were tipsy with victory. I couldn't believe that I had had the neurotic foresight to never join social media. I watched the people around me scroll the hate-chatter, widen their eyes in horror, and then shove their phones into pockets with a subject change. "Do you um . . . what's your . . . how's . . . let's get bagels!"

I felt sick, like the Monday feeling after Saturday cocaine and two packs of Camels. Like your stomach is an open trash can with old, infected rain in it. Like you went to a Metallica concert and hugged the front-row amp for three hours and are now at a 6:00 a.m. Civil War lecture. Not even real pain, just gross, empty, chemical numbness.

In an attempt to put an ant's Band-Aid on the mammoth hemorrhaging narrative, I did a morning talk show. It was the kind where you have to get there at dawn and wrap your tits in linens, balance on an eight-foot stool, and tell a cutesy story about traffic. But I missed Seacrest's cue for my rush hour story, and I stumbled over a preplanned pun. World hunger took a back seat to the pain of this misstep. I was no longer an upright person but a human circle, up my own ass to the shoulders in *poor me*. I felt the Palace doors closing.

I rode home to Brooklyn in toxic narcissism, bathing in the acid of my downfall. I glazed over the tens of incoming panic texts. All-caps emails flew back and forth, the hysteria of The Business bleeding into my brain that this all really, *really* mattered. I pulled up to my house in sobs. I lamented to the driver that I didn't have cash for a tip since this was a borrowed (bejeweled, pony-shaped) purse, confused why his eyes weren't filled with understanding pity.

Still in my borrowed fancy linens and full-bridal ghoul makeup, I took Babe for a walk.

But we didn't walk anymore. We rolled. Babe's disease had progressed to the point where he needed wheels, his back legs now like a little broken sled that he dragged around the apartment. A little furry porcine merman, breaking your heart with his human smile that would apparently be the last thing to go.

Soaking in my cloud of sad, I began the new routine. I engaged my spray-tanned core and heaved the dead weight of his fifty pounds from the floor to my chest. I carried his leaden-lamb body down the three flights of stairs to the street. I hooked his leash to the gate. Still in antifeminist velvet platforms, I ran back up the stoop stairs to grab his wheels, swearing at my calf-spasms as I bounced. Poor, poor Betty. I stopped at the top of the stairs in a sob and gave a Veruca Salt stomp. Why was this happening to me? I had fought for and done the impossible thing—where was my promised parade? Babe harrumphed from the street. *I'm coming, I'm coming.* I tore the row of fake lashes that my tears had dislodged and threw them to the ground.

I crouched next to Babe and paused. He snarfed. I remembered the absurd number on the price tag digging into my back. Babe whimpered, but I needed a second. I couldn't fuck up this fancy, not-mine shirt. I took a few moments to roll up my silk sleeves. I guided his defunct back legs into the insane contraption, whose commercial promised us would fix everything, but of course he hated it. My phone dinged repeatedly, more panic texts, updates about the movie's spectacular misconception roiling across the interweb. An alum from my middle school helpfully texted me a meme of my face. "Is this really you?? U OK?? LOL." I wondered how Jonah got my number as I fumbled with the twisted straps, a misaligned latch. *This sucks, this sucks for me.* I was told this would be my coronation, and it's my execution. Pig's blood dripped on my crown from the rafters. The Palace was turning on me, and I didn't even get to go to one ball.

Sometimes a sign comes as a burst of sunlight through a cottage window. Sometimes it's a dead aunt's favorite ABBA song filtering into a diner. Sometimes, simply, it's a squirt.

I had waited too long. My tantrum on the landing and sigh on the pavement took time the boy couldn't afford. Babe's butthole function had quit the project a few weeks ago and was now a sort of fickle Vesuvius underscoring our lives. It chose now.

Babe's colon erupted in liquid *no*. Shit poured all over the absurd white sailor pant I was told was a brand to watch. A geyser of feces here to spackle my designer thighs on the street. A group of gentlemen enjoying an early morning brown-bagged lager screamed the collective reaction vowel of a Maury paternity test reveal.

"OOOOOOOOOOOOOH!"

"FUCK!" I screamed.

Babe's eyes darted up to me. The look that a dog gives you where suddenly you want to kill yourself. We stared at each other, frozen in our New York "stations of the cross" tableau. Babe. My sweetest boy. His honey-clown eyes that had a million times before rolled at my practicing fake tears, blinked asleep across the room on Cosmo's chest, and stared into mine asking for help with a gross thing. As they did now. Help me, Mom. I need your help.

I sat down next to him and hugged him, piss-soaked and shaking, into the stupid fucking silk. I kissed his block head. I scratched his golden salty feather ears. I took my manicured hand that tomboy-me would scoff at, that had spent the day scrolling desperately for validation. But now I was awake. That was not my hand's highest purpose that day. It was this. As the vet told us would need to happen eventually: I took my finger and put it in Babe's butt. To help him shit.

A man the size of an oak tree with a gun in his waistband John-Wayned by.

A specific cloud went over his face, the one betraying canine history. He kept his eyes on the ground as he passed, then quietly choked the only thing that mattered at all.

"Das love."

20

OH WOW THE END

When I was six, I stood on top of a red velvet seat that I remember being in the second row, but perhaps this is convenient editing because that seat sounds expensive. Whatever row it was, I stood on it and screamed. The crotch of my church tights sagged low like a clown's pants. I reached my hands in Beatlemania glee at the row of dancers in front of me, the cast of *Crazy for You* swanning through their encore. My mom grabbed my tiny shoulder and pointed at the lead, a man in tails inexplicably pointing back at . . . me. He clapped, laughing toward me, as if to say, *And bravo to* you. Apparently I had been so maniacal in my response to my first Broadway show that I had warranted a nod at the curtain call. To this day, listening to a show tune where suddenly the sound of a million tap shoes rains its joyful Morse code into my headphones, I cry and have to call my mom.

My mom, the woman who flicks away societal *shouldn't*s like mosquitos. Who, as a girl, shrouded her beloved sister Mary in an overcoat like a tweed ghost and ran her screaming through the first floor of the Museum of Natural History, saddle shoes thundering past the dinosaur skeleton that terrified Mary, because my mom knew she'd love the rest. My mom who once made like she was going to turn left into the school parking lot and then swung a terrifying minivan-lurching right, careening like a police chase onto the empty soccer field. My brothers and I screamed from the back in harmonizing mortification. I was twelve, and the wrong gloss hue was suicide; a maniacal Mommed school entrance was burning your popularity draft card. She ignored my screams. She turned the radio up and rolled the windows down. I remember her flicking her eyes up at me in the rearview mirror, eyebrow arching for a second. I see now that it was a quantum wave, a message to my future self. Then I was horrified, but now I know exactly what she was doing: enjoying a moment of trapdoor-less id. Pure unposing *fuck it*. She tore up the Montessori field with Dodge Caravan donuts, kicking Everyone Wins mud into the sky. She wailed along to her favorite song. *Oh Happy Day*. She swerved huge *S*'s toward the goal until our protests turned to obliging belts.

He taught me hooooooooow! To waaaatch! Fight and pray. Fight and pray!

Prodded through time by future me, I stopped sulking and sang at my mom, her Connemara-orange hair whipping into tangles, barefoot-flooring the gas pedal across the grass.

Years later in that same soccer field in the middle of the night, I had a screaming fight and drove home drunk, like an idiot. The other half of the screams followed me, drunker, and screamed more screams from the bottom of my driveway as my family slept. I ran down through snow in a miniskirt to tell Max, finally, I was a towering human monster, not a minuscule tissue. But I lost my courage and turned back around, screaming it silently instead at a tree that a decade later a different boy would cut down to make a headboard.

The boy whom I would later walk down the aisle toward through crying friends, many of whom were former diapered-and-training-bra-ed alphas whose shine taught me shining doesn't kill you. Most were people I met the best way you can meet someone, pinching each other in backstage dark, then under the lights making Kryptonite eye contact when someone in row B farts. I walked arm in arm with my parents, the carnie people who raised me to find joy and questions wherever I could, and whenever possible, funny hats. A bow-tied beast trotted behind with the rings, harrumphing in boredom at the bottom of my dress throughout the ceremony. A dress that hours later on the dance floor, the drunk women who built me helped me chop short with kitchen scissors, freeing my legs from the patriarchy, or maybe just so I could kick higher to Prince.

In all my running from myself, it is hard to remember that I also love the thing I'm running from. That I'm in all this for the big feelings. I don't want them to be muted. Not really. But when I feel them, I feel them all the way, and the ground opens and that's terrifying. The Salem feelings are less predictable, less controllable. Scarier. The Barbie stuff is smaller but easier, more numb. Safer. Those lows aren't as deep and harrowing. But the moments that have felt like my cells explode into liquid sugar and I'm sobbing in a *thank you* to the sky have nothing to do with approval or victory. Not from love—from loving.

So the movie was cancelled and my dog was sick. I put my phone away, just turned it off, because I realized this was the end. And though I had fought to learn to be a protagonist, it was now my job to tase my pride and listen. Because now the boy needed me, to say goodbye to the other boy.

No one wants to read about a dog dying. I'll make it quick. We went to the country and sat on the porch and fed him blueberries. A pixie-cutted veterinarian with a Demi Moore voice came to the house and talked too much, although silence would have been terrible, too. After it was done, the vet referred to Babe as "she," and we later joked darkly that the vet was not a vet but a serial pet killer who'd hacked our phones, and the *real* vet would pull up after she left. But right now there was no joking. We carried him to her car together, Cosmo cradling one of the great loves of his life. We walked him past the irises that he closed his eyes to touch his nose to every morning. Because Babe was good at what we were not—peace. Breathing in the peace of the world.

We watched the car drive away. I turned around into a moment so powerful that I could feel it punch itself forever onto the memory grid. Cosmo's eyes were the bluest they'd ever been, spilling out at me the idiot, the fool who almost took all this excruciating beauty for granted. He crumpled into me, and I held him, both of us bracing at the tidal wave toll of loving something too much. The greatest, most horrible honor there is.

Six months later, when the world had forgotten five times over and the nation's brain had Etch a Sketch reset and a phone call came, I barely shrugged. My DNA felt different. Tired and older and freer. But *this is it,* they told me. All was forgiven or forgotten or just no one cared anymore. *The Hunt* was coming out.

A small press tour ensued, a junket where we did interviews

detailing the film's assured phoenix narrative. I released the essay I'd written half a year ago in self-important sobs, the one I was told would be met with pitchforks. It was now met with . . . crickets. The internet had new battles a thousand times over. Vitriol is loud; redemption is mute. We laughed through the irony that where there had been air horns there were now yawns.

I tried insisting to my friends that I was post-epiphany and I'd go alone, but Patrick refused to let the moment pass and talked me into making the premiere a group date. Perspective epiphany or not, it was still a big deal in our little world, and we should at least toast to the moment and laugh at the trajectory. Usually I wore tight *please-God-hire-me-before-I-expire* Lycra tubes on the red carpet, ever cognizant that each photo could be my last chance to advertise goods that were about to curdle. That seemed exhausting now. I wore a black suit. Instead of a steely, fellatey squint face, I smiled big in the pictures like it was my pizza party. I told Cosmo we'd go to the after-party for *one* drink. I had work the next morning. *GLOW,* a job I loved. I had scene ideas I didn't want to be tired for.

The theatre was half-empty, which my friends made fun of me for, which is how you know you have the right friends. But when the lights dimmed, they punched my arms in giddy we-did-it, which is having the right friends, too. Stoned and cramming Girl Scout cookies in their faces, they screamed and laughed and breathed at all the right parts.

And then that scene came. I realized in all the insanity I'd forgotten about my little improvisation experiment and was suddenly nervous to see what ended up in the film. Despite a decade of disappointment boot camp, I held my breath in hope.

They used it. There it was, the weird little hum moment, the entire improvised thing. It's just a fifteen-second part of a movie, and it feels lame to mention and lamer still to explain, but . . . I don't know. For me, it's it. I got to have the moment happen. In a once-disgraced, now-forgotten movie, to a half-empty theatre. But the scene played, and for just a *second* the air changed, like it does in a play sometimes. Patrick turned to me teary and faux-angry. A girlfriend mouthed a modern *I See You and I'm Proud*: "GO. *FUCK*. YOURSELF." A bald suit in the second row turned and looked back at me. I heard a breathy "wow" from a stranger. Cosmo squeezed my shoulder.

And then—I *saw* it. The tiny light.

A real one, appearing like a fairy, right in the center of the front row. Gleaming up at me, sparkling hello for the one second it would last.

The tiny light.

Of a cell phone.

Your dream comes true. The world flickers in recognition. Then checks its email.

It happened, though. No trumpets, no lightning. I looked at my hands, and they looked the same. But it was nice.

The movie came out in theatres on a Friday.

Friday, the thirteenth.

Of March.

March.

. . . 2020.

It played to empty theatres for two days. Then, of course, as everything was, it was gone by Sunday.

———

The following Tuesday I walked into the kitchen holding a stick with two lines. When Cosmo turned to me, he was already crying, having received the secret through the back of his head. Months later he took my picture in front of a theatre. I posed in an N95 mask, one hand on my huge belly, the other pointing at the towering movie poster no one had bothered to take down.

Resting my swelling feet in quarantine, I scrolled through society's attempt at a cultural shift from self to unity. Posts of arched backs and duck lips were paired with captions of Rūmī and Seuss. *We're gonna get thru this 2gether, also look at my butt.* Movie stars streamed an attempt at shared quarantine boredom, riffing in labyrinthian home gyms and Olympic pools, a forgotten novelty pet shitting in the background. Judgment Day has come, and we are an heiress's neglected piglet in a grAtiTUde tee. I am Jack's shaved mini horse.

We agreed not to find out the baby's sex, if only to infuse *some* excitement in an era that was so Groundhog Blegh. But Gilpins were never girls except me, and I whispered to friends that I thought it was a boy. I was also pretty sure the ultrasound tech slipped up at six months and said, "He's . . . *it's* . . . looking great." It being a pandemic and no dads allowed in the appointments, I was smug with secret knowledge.

I spent 2020 waddling around shuttered New York. I had phone dates with every girl and woman whom I'd ever skipped or smoked with. Marie and I texted, exchanging paragraphs as we had when we were nine-year-old pen pals. In an "oh my God

I'm going be a bad mom" panic, I called Bunny. She was a doula now and a mom of two. She told me everything was going to be OK. She sent me books and jokes. Dani told me in a stern voice what foods to avoid. Bunny told me to eat them anyway.

I shook my head at all the wasted time. All the time I feared and worshipped women who were just in pain, too. It's a cancer on forward movement. We are all in the same dumb pink woman-circus, having to develop in reverse, presenting a final self in act 1 and admitting at the curtain call we don't know who we are. Bunny's bite was the same as my bow, just trying to beat rejection to the punch. We all just use different methods. Easy to write off hers as heresy if it doesn't look like yours. Maybe that's why it's easy to be a blanket feminist, but turn away from the actualizers on your front lawn. Ugh. If society comes back, I'll try to do less of that.

The wasted time hating my body. My body that was now not posing and shrinking but sorcerizing and expanding. I'd spent decades treating it like a Tamagotchi, and now I saw it was a NASA supercomputer all along. The moral of the story is *not* Every Woman Should Have a Baby—*fuck* no. The moral is we are capable of cauldron shit. So proceed accordingly. The cycled selves and darkness and wonder . . . all of these are powers. What we are told is shameful or cute are actually fucking powers. We just have to stop using them to hurt ourselves. Point your barrel from your temple to the sky.

I rubbed my belly. I hoped the person in there wouldn't waste the time hating themselves that I did. Maybe the amount I already loved them, they could borrow? Was self-love like forgetting toothpaste at camp?

Speaking of cauldron shit: the trapdoor. Impending mother-hood made it feel less like a steel cover and more like a flimsy screen. I suspected the baby's arrival would blow it off its hinges entirely. Maybe the Salem and Barbie inhabitants would meet each other, warted claw shaking French-manicured hand. Maybe together they could teach me how best to be a woman.

An aimless walk took me to Eleventh Street. A sharply dressed teddy bear in a brownstone window seemed hauntingly familiar, and I called my mom.

"Yep," she said through a Peppermint Pattie. "He's been there for thirty years, in different outfits according to season. We used to point him out on the way to the playground."

After we hung up, she texted me a YouTube link to a perfor-mance of *42nd Street,* and I realized we'd spent solo pandemic time the same way: sniffling along to old show tunes. I blasted Jerry Orbach's tenor into my headphones and walked faster and faster up Sixth Avenue, until I was pounding my feet into the cement with joy.

COOOOOME AAAAA-LONG, COME ON ALONG AND LISTEN TO

THE LULLABY OF BROADWAY

The week of Thanksgiving I reached down and lifted up every-thing I'd run from and looked in its face. I inhaled in the shock of my life then laughed choking at the dumb, dumb, obvious truth that my "nightmare" was of course the thing I wanted most of all. It looked right through to the center of me, screaming, and I screamed back. A girl.

We named her after my mom's favorite person because my

mom is mine. We also named her after the thing that taught *me* to be a mom, and that peace and joy and pain are honors if you let them be. And they're more blinding and beautiful than any quick flicker of tiny light.

It's one of the things I will try my best to teach Mary Babe.

ACKNOWLEDGMENTS

Thank you to no one, I did it myself!

Nope, I'm receiving word from science that the only reason this book exists is other people carried me like a lead baby.

Thank you to my friends. I would be dead if you didn't exist. Not hyperbole, just law. I love you. Specifically thank you to Zoe, Rightor, Cristin, Rebecca, Lela, and Scotty for reading drafts of this book and being filtered-honest, as requested.

Thank you to my family. Someone once described our family as "a bunch of people walking around in bathrobes hugging each other." Thank you for letting me write about us. Sam and Harry and Blair, I love you more than is humanly possible. And to my sister, Gladys, *fuck you.* (There is no Gladys! This is fun.)

Thank you to Bryn Clark at Flatiron for making me feel understood and for teaching me the wild theory that my *sentences* should be understood, too. Thank you, Bryn, for everything.

Thank you to Kristyn Keene Benton at ICM, who somehow knew that I was never going to begin to write this book without a years-long gentle nudging campaign. Kristyn, your patience is impressive. Thank you.

Thank you, Jennifer Rappaport, for copyediting a grammatical war crime. I salute your bravery.

Thank you, Meghan Houser, for your insight. It helped me so much.

Thank you to Dara Gordon, Tony Lipp, Sean Liebowitz, everyone at Anonymous, and ICM. Thank you Jenny Tversky, John Meigs, Katherine McClure.

Thank you to post-baby hormones that told me *keep writing this seems like a good idea whatever! Life is a cabaret!* Thank you self for not deleting the entire thing when later hormones told you to do that. Many, many, *many* times.

Thank you to people I haven't met yet who will confuse our history and be mad they're not on this list.

Thank you to YOU, for being so fully *with* a book to the end that you read the acknowledgments. I can't say I've ever read them myself.

Thank you, Babe. Thank you, MB.

Thanks, Cos.

ABOUT THE AUTHOR

Betty Gilpin is an Emmy, Critic's Choice, and SAG Award–nominated actress and writer whose credits include *GLOW, Gaslit,* and *Three Women,* among others. She has—bravely—fake cried and fake died on your television with many different grasping-at-relevance hair colors. The blonde giveth, and the ginger taketh away. Her essays have been published in *The New York Times, Glamour, Lenny Letter, The Hollywood Reporter,* and *Vanity Fair.*